JEROME AND ROHWER

Jerome and Rohwer

Memories of Japanese American Internment
in World War II Arkansas

Edited by Walter M. Imahara and David E. Meltzer

The University of Arkansas Press
Fayetteville | 2022

978-1-68226-188-0 (cloth)
978-1-68226-241-2 (paperback)
978-1-61075-759-1 (electronic)

27 26 25 24 23   5 4 3 2 1

Manufactured in the United States of America

Designed by Liz Lester

♾ The paper used in this publication meets the minimum requirements of the American National Standard for Permanence of Paper for Printed Library Materials Z39.48-1984.

Library of Congress Cataloging-in-Publication Data

Names: Imahara, Walter M., editor. | Meltzer, David E., editor.
Title: Jerome and Rohwer: memories of Japanese American internment in World War II Arkansas / edited by Walter M. Imahara and David E. Meltzer.
Description: Fayetteville: The University of Arkansas Press, 2022. | Includes index. | Summary: "Collection of autobiographical remembrances related to life in the Jerome and Rohwer Japanese American internment camps during World War II"—Provided by publisher.
Identifiers: LCCN 2021021839 (print) | LCCN 2021021840 (ebook) | ISBN 9781682261880 (cloth) | ISBN 9781610757591 (ebook)
Subjects: LCSH: Japanese Americans—Evacuation and relocation, 1942–1945. | World War, 1939–1945—Personal narratives, American. | World War, 1939–1945—Japanese Americans—Biography. | World War, 1939–1945—Concentration camps—Arkansas. | LCGFT: Personal narratives.| Biographies.
Classification: LCC D769.8.A6 J47 2022 (print) | LCC D769.8.A6 (ebook) | DDC 940.53/17767850923956—dc23
LC record available at https://lccn.loc.gov/2021021839
LC ebook record available at https://lccn.loc.gov/2021021840

Title page, top photo: Jerome Relocation Center, Denson, Arkansas, 1944. *Charles E. Mace; War Relocation Authority Photo, National Archives Collection.*

Bottom photo: Jerome Relocation Center, Denson, Arkansas, 1942. *Tom Parker; War Relocation Authority Photo, National Archives Collection.*

Dedicated to all former internees in the Jerome and Rohwer
Relocation Centers in Arkansas, 1942–1945;
to my father, James Masaru Imahara;
and to my mother, Haruka Sunada Imahara.

—WALTER M. IMAHARA

CONTENTS

I have known and loved the remarkable Imahara family for nearly fifty years now, and it was my privilege to ghostwrite the autobiography of its patriarch, the late James M. Imahara, who was proud to call his book *Son of Immigrants*. Our preliminary interviews were the first time he had spoken about the trauma and struggles of the war and internment, and the outpouring of emotion was heart-wrenching. I hope the book was as cathartic for him as it was scary for me, but he told me I'd better get everything he said once, because he was never talking about it again. I realized he meant that when I accompanied him to the local book club for a review. He wouldn't say a single word about the book or his experiences, but, looking around the room at the audience of mostly portly matrons, he whipped off his sports coat and started showing them exercises he did to remain in such good shape in his old age. I don't believe I ever took him with me to another book club!

His son Walter went in many different directions, but he never could stop planting. That green thumb he inherited was never satisfied if he wasn't planning and planting and maintaining some fabulous garden or other. After he retired from the family's very successful nursery in Baton Rouge, Walter spent years turning a cow pasture into a botanical wonderland to be shared with historic St. Francisville's many visitors, then developed a gorgeous arboretum, and he's just finished a legacy garden at the Hemingbough cultural center—and who knows what he'll do next.

Besides his horticultural skills, Walter and his lovely wife Sumi are consummate hosts, and their annual New Year's Eve party was a fabulous experience. Their guests always came from such different realms and rarely knew each other, but Walter would make each one stand up and tell the story of their acquaintance and involvement with him and his family, and it made for such lively conversations.

Walter Imahara's story is such an interesting one, starting with a shamefully misguided event and chronicling his great effort and stubborn determination to succeed—and succeed he did. And a tip of the hat to his brave mother for saving the scrapbooks of vintage family photos when she had to leave behind so many other possessions during internment; they add so much to the Imahara story.

ANNE BUTLER
St. Francisville, Louisiana

———

I have only known Walter for a few short years. And during that time, I loved learning his and his family's story. That is the purpose of this book.

During World War II, more than one hundred twenty thousand Japanese Americans were incarcerated and sent to camps from California to Arkansas. Many of these same people share their stories herein.

I was one that never knew about internment. It was not taught when I was in school in Arkansas, and I learned about this part of our history only when I started at the WWII Japanese American Internment Museum in McGehee, Arkansas, where I was curator from 2013 to 2021. My knee-jerk reaction was, "What? What, Arkansas for goodness' sake!" It has been an amazing journey for me over the past six years for what I have learned and am still learning.

At one of the reunions of former Jerome/Rohwer internees a few years ago, Walter spoke. I found his story to be amazing, and I am so looking forward to reading his compilation of stories from the camps.

Nidoto Nai Yoni—Let it not happen again.

SUSAN GALLION
McGehee, Arkansas

———

As chairman of the WWII Japanese American Internment Museum in McGehee, Arkansas, I feel honored to contribute to this foreword on behalf of my friend Mr. Walter Imahara.

In April 2013, the museum opened, and to date we have had more than sixteen thousand visitors come through. The grand opening, which was taped by the *CBS Morning Show*, had George Takei as our special guest of ceremonies, and he gave a very touching story about his time at the Rohwer camp. The City of McGehee's support, which has generated several thousand dollars in donations, has been overwhelming. We have had people from all over the country call us to donate items of interest that they have had from that period, in the hope that we might showcase them. While we have undertaken the creation of this museum, we have had a great deal of support from different organizations that are putting forth their time to enhance the museum.

This book will illuminate and intensify the emotional, personal human stories that often get lost in the standard historical presentation, as this history has gone unnoticed long enough. I feel it's a story that needs to be told, as the Japanese American internment experience is an important chapter in American history.

JEFF OWYOUNG
Mayor of McGehee and chairman
of the World War II Japanese
American Internment Museum

PREFACE

This book is an extraordinary, practically unique document, for it is—to our knowledge—the only work composed of autobiographical remembrances solely related to life in the Jerome and Rohwer Relocation Centers in Arkansas written by former internees and their immediate families. It is one of the very few collections of postwar reminiscences devoted to a single one or two of the ten wartime relocation camps, and it is one of the *very* few books to collect in a single volume the firsthand experiences of former internees in their own writing. (Most of the few otherwise similar books comprise oral histories or excerpts from oral histories.) As it is now more than seventy-five years since the camps were closed down, it may be assumed that the present volume is one of the last of its kind that will ever be produced. It is, in many ways, a unique document of the wartime years in the state of Arkansas and, indeed, the entire United States.

The book is a collection of brief autobiographical memoirs written by former internees and their close family members. Many of these accounts were written specifically for this book, while others were written years ago and have been collected here for the first time. The collection was edited by Walter Imahara, one of the former internees represented in the book, as well as by myself. The memoirs focus on the war years, including the time following the attack on Pearl Harbor, the rounding up and forced relocation of the entire West Coast Japanese American population, and the years spent in the camps. The former internees—almost all of those still alive now are in their eighties or nineties—have many vivid memories of those years, and most of their stories are accompanied by photographs and other illustrations related to these life-changing experiences.

It has been my pleasure and my honor to assist in bringing this book to publication. We are fortunate that Walter Imahara came up with the idea for this book, and equally fortunate that he found such an enthusiastic reception for the idea among his fellow former internees, who then proceeded to set down their recollections with clarity and attention to detail. Their writings and family photographs bring to life the experiences of involuntary incarceration in a way that no other historical writing can fully capture. The result is a vivid and indelible document of a terrible time in US history, and it will contribute to ensuring that what happened during those years will never be forgotten.

DAVID E. MELTZER
Mesa, Arizona

ACKNOWLEDGMENTS

Initial editing of contributors' submissions was done by Sumi Imahara, who also helped throughout the later stages of the editing process. Initial typesetting, layout, and formatting of the preliminary version of the book were done by Jamie Dupre. Cover art design for a special proof copy of the book distributed to contributors was created by Amy Metz Hebert. Tom Stroman provided expert assistance during the final phase of proofreading, and the index was created by PJ Heim.

This is the only known photo that shows Walter Imahara and his entire family in the internment camps. Taken in the Jerome Relocation Center, the photo shows Walter's father James Imahara at the far right, holding Walter's sister Irene. Then, in sequence from right to left, is younger brother John, Walter himself, sister Lily, a person unknown, and Walter's mother Haruka holding his brother Jun. At the right in the second row, above James, is Walter's sister Flora; then, going right to left, are his sisters May and Jane.

INTRODUCTION

This is a book about remembrances of being an internee at the Jerome and Rohwer relocation camps in Arkansas during World War II. I was not an internee, I am not of Japanese American heritage, and I was born after World War II had ended. Although I vaguely remembered hearing stories about the war, it meant nothing to me when I was a child. Still, I came to realize, as a fifth-generation Californian, I do have memories of internees' stories. It wasn't until I was asked to contribute to the introduction to this book that they started to meld into my story.

The relocation of Japanese Americans during World War II is a big part of the history of California but, as a small girl growing up in South Pasadena, I had little understanding of the event. I remember we had a gardener named Tommy Matsuoka, whom my parents adored, and they often went to his home for Japanese dinners. I now realize that probably most Japanese gardeners in Southern California in the 1950s had been internees, as were the parents and other relatives of my Japanese American friends. Even then I was well aware of the Manzanar camp along US Route 395 near Lone Pine. Route 395 is the only road that runs along the eastern side of the Sierra Nevada mountain range, and any trip from Los Angeles north to Reno, Nevada, and points beyond had to pass by Manzanar, still visible after being closed down in 1945. We traveled this road several times a year, and my folks would always point out the camp, which was very close to the road and had rock pillars at the entrance. My parents had driven this road all their lives before the war. My dad was stationed at Wendover, Utah, with the Army Air Corps during the war, so every trip from South Pasadena to Utah passed by the active camp.

In 2015, I moved from Southern California to Clovis, a city that adjoins Fresno in Central California, and there I joined the Westerners International historical group. As we approached 2017, the seventy-fifth anniversary of Executive Order 9066 that authorized the removal and internment of Japanese Americans, the group hosted several programs on the history of the Japanese American community in the Central Valley and the numerous temporary assembly centers for internees that were housed at fairgrounds in the region. Fresno had two: one at Fresno County Fairgrounds and one at an old lumber mill named Pinedale. I began to realize how much the Japanese internment was an integral part of the fabric of this great agricultural area. I became aware of memorials to the internees in the Fresno area, built to remind people of the injustices . that happened here.

In 2016, after settling into my new community, I booked a trip on a paddle-wheel riverboat on the mighty Mississippi River from Memphis to New Orleans. One of our stops was in St. Francisville, Louisiana, a wonderful, quaint historic town near Baton Rouge. I met and became friends with some local people and have made several return visits. I subsequently learned of Imahara's Botanical Garden in St. Francisville, and my friend said he thought the Imaharas were originally from California. I googled the botanical garden and found the whole Imahara family story. They were most certainly from California! The family with seven children had been uprooted from Sacramento and sent to the Fresno Assembly Center, where an eighth child was born. They were all then sent on to the relocation camps called Jerome and Rohwer, in Arkansas. James Imahara, the father, had been born in Watsonville, California, in 1903, so all of his children were second-generation American citizens. The Imaharas' story is unique, because when they were released, they did not return to California, but chose to go to New Orleans. Thinking that postwar prejudices and racism might be less severe in the South, the family with nine children (the ninth born in 1947) found themselves isolated in an area with virtually no other Asian faces, no community support. What a culture shock! Especially for the children, who had just spent three and a half years in a camp with all Japanese faces. With sheer guts, determination, and centuries-old Japanese traditions, the family ultimately thrived and sent eight of their nine children to college. It took a little doing!

On one trip to St. Francisville in 2018, I was standing in front of my friend's house when I saw a white pickup, with "Imahara's Landscaping" emblazoned on the side, driving down the main street. I flagged down the driver, stuck my head in the passenger window, and said, "You don't know me, but I'm from Fresno and I know your story!" That was how I met Walter Imahara.

Shortly after that visit, Valley PBS in Fresno aired their documentary, *Silent Sacrifice*, which was originally only broadcast for a Central Valley viewership. The documentary covered the history of immigrants in the Central Valley and the internment at Fresno Assembly Center, where internees were housed in horse stables. The film highlighted a couple from Fresno who had been children at the camp in Rohwer and had met and married in Fresno. The production crew took this couple back to Arkansas and filmed their reactions to returning there, more than seventy-five years later. I was surprised to learn that so many from Fresno were sent so far. As I watched this great documentary, I thought, "This is the Imahara story, but they will never see it because it is only being broadcast in the Central Valley."

When I went to St. Francisville for Thanksgiving in 2018, I took a DVD of *Silent Sacrifice* with me. I called Walter and said, "You probably don't remember me, but about a year ago I stopped your truck on Ferdinand Street and introduced myself." Walter invited me to his office/ museum in Baton Rouge and I brought him the DVD. I had a delightful visit with him and his brother John. At his office he has about two hundred haiku plaques, with Japanese characters hand-carved into cypress boards. This constitutes about half of the collection done by his father, James Imahara, in his retirement.

That day I became a member of the Imaharas' extended family. Walter was so moved by the film about the internees, that within twenty-four hours of my sharing it he had added me to a family group email of about twenty people telling them of my wonderful gift of this extraordinary film about their life! He was especially excited about the pictures of the horse stalls at Fresno Assembly Center, which had obviously been seared into his five-year-old mind in 1942.

On Christmas night 2018, I heard a text come in around 10 p.m., and it was from Walter in Louisiana, where it was midnight. He said he was watching the film with his brother-in-law and they were fast-forwarding it to the end, because he saw one of his father's haiku plaques and he wanted to take a picture of it on the TV screen. I told him to send it to me when he got it. In a few minutes, I received a text with a picture of the plaque on TV and a picture of a very somber Walter standing by his Christmas-decorated dining table. The text read, "Shelley. Got the photo of my father's haiku board that was given to the McGehee museum in 2017. Wow, my father's haiku is in the film. I will now send to the family. Thanks so much. Walt." Then, a few minutes later: "Shelley. I just sent text and photos to nine family members. Tonight, Christmas, I found the haiku photo and I am a bit emotional. Wow, best gift I ever received. Thanks to you. Wow. Hospital chimney at Jerome, Ark. Photo from DVD. Thanks." This is the only plaque to have left the family collection. The documentary producers had filmed it at the museum and had used it in the closing montage of *Silent Sacrifice*. Only a few people in the entire world would recognize that plaque, in that film, made so far away in California. It was truly a night of miracles—a story of so many random events that combined to complete a life's story. Or maybe they aren't so random after all!

I was also overcome with emotion, to realize that I could so profoundly influence another person's life and that of his family, by simply stepping out and flagging down a stranger. It has been an overwhelming example of how tiny the degree of separation between all humans actually is.

Walter and his wife, Sumi, were going to attend an internee reunion on July 5, 2019, in San Jose, and I encouraged them to visit Fresno while they were in California. In all of his world travels, Walter had never been back to Fresno since leaving in 1942 for Arkansas as a five-year-old. That's seventy-seven years! They stayed for two days with family in Fresno for the first time, and I arranged for a twelve-passenger van to carry our little group around. I gathered local experts, who are now friends, to tell the narrative of the Central Valley's role in Japanese American internment, and we visited the memorials and museums that preserve that legacy. I also arranged for Valley Public Radio to interview Walter and other internees at the Fresno Assembly Center Memorial, located at the Fresno Fairgrounds. A huge bronze plaque at the Memorial lists the names of all 5,344 individuals who were incarcerated at the Assembly Center from May to October 1942. Our interviewer, Laura Tsutsui, had grandparents who were internees, and she found their names on the monument. She was trying to interview Walter as he found and read the names of his family on that same monument. Walter was filled with emotion as he read all the names of his family members. This type of memorial is so emotional when you visit it with someone who lived it. The guided tour through my newly adopted city was as much a learning experience for me as it was for Walter and his family. The timing, being July 2 and 3, was another coincidence in this convoluted tale. Visiting the sites of confinement, which stole people's freedom, on the eve of the Fourth of July, our celebration of freedom, had a sense of irony to it. Yet for many people, finally getting some closure to certain times in their life is freeing in itself.

I flagged Walter down on Ferdinand Street; I brought him *Silent Sacrifice* at Thanksgiving; he saw his father's haiku plaque on Christmas;

and he toured the sites of his confinement on the eve of the Fourth of July. To quote Robert Frost, I took the road less traveled, and that has made all the difference!

SHELLEY FETTERMAN
Clovis, California

———————

It was on July 2, 2019, that I had the privilege of meeting Walter Imahara and his lovely wife, Sumi, who were in Fresno, California, to visit the Fresno Assembly Center Memorial, the site in the Fresno Fairgrounds where the Imahara family was interned at the start of World War II.

After meeting Walter, I found out that we had so much in common, being that we were the same age; both of our families at the start of World War II were interned in an assembly center that was used as a temporary internment camp in California; both of us were later transferred to permanent concentration camps in Arkansas.

Walter's family was from Northern California and was sent to the Fresno Fairgrounds assembly center in 1942. The Imaharas were living in horse stables until being transferred to a concentration camp in Jerome, Arkansas, and later being moved to the concentration camp in Rohwer, Arkansas, upon the closing of Jerome to make room for German prisoners of war.

Our Saito family was from Southern California and, at the start of World War II, was sent to an assembly center at the Santa Anita racetrack, where we also lived in horse stables until we were transferred to a concentration camp in Rohwer, Arkansas.

Although the Imahara and Saito families never met while in Rohwer, seventy-seven years later Walter Imahara and I met in Fresno, California, and became close friends, sharing our memories of the evacuation and internment of our families during World War II.

Walter's family never returned to their roots in Florin, California, after the war, instead moving to Baton Rouge, Louisiana, where they started a nursery and landscape business. During this time Walter designed and developed the Imahara Legacy Garden in St. Francisville to honor members of his family. In contrast, the Saito family returned to their home in Montebello, California, and my father worked for Star Nurseries and later opened the family's Saito Garden Center.

While Walter was developing Imahara's Nursery and Landscape Company, I became a landscape architect and worked for the Los Angeles and Anaheim parks and recreation departments, designing parks and public buildings. My first assignment for the City of Anaheim was to prepare the landscape plans for Anaheim Stadium, followed by landscape plans for the Anaheim Convention Center, which is located across the street from Disneyland.

Upon entering private practice in 1972, I was commissioned by the City of Fresno to design the Shinzen Japanese Garden in Woodward Park. Isn't it an interesting coincidence that while Walter was developing Imahara's Legacy Garden, with a Japanese theme, in St. Francisville, I was developing the Shinzen Japanese Garden in Fresno?

After reviewing Walter's history, I find we share so many similarities including spending over three years in concentration camps in Arkansas; serving in the military (Walter in the army, and I in the air force); designing and developing Japanese gardens for the public to enjoy; and both being Christians.

The Japanese community in Fresno has contributed to the important history of the Japanese internment by developing two assembly center memorials in Fresno, California. The first is called Remembrance Plaza and is located in the northern section of Fresno, where over five thousand internees from Washington, Oregon, and Sacramento were interned in the Pinedale Assembly Center. The second is the Fresno Assembly Center Memorial located on the Fresno Fairgrounds, where over five thousand internees from Fresno County were interned.

This portrait of Walter Imahara is a true reflection of both of our lives, as well as those of the other one hundred and twenty thousand Japanese Americans who were interned in assembly centers and concentration camps during World War II.

This is an important time in American history that should not be forgotten or left out of history books. It reflects all the sacrifices that Japanese Americans endured during World War II fighting prejudice at home while Nisei solders fought and sacrificed their lives overseas so that all Americans could be safe and free.

PAUL SAITO
Fresno, California

JEROME AND ROHWER

Russell Endo

My Mother's Words

During World War II, my family was imprisoned at Santa Anita and Jerome. While there my mother, Yoshiko, wrote a series of letters to Violet Sell, a former teacher. These provide descriptions of her experiences as they were happening. Below, excerpts from these letters are interwoven with written notes my mother sent to me in September 1975. The article concludes with a portion of her testimony for the Redress Commission in 1981. My editorial additions appear in brackets [].

Yoshiko Hanato was born in East San Pedro in 1919 and was the elder of the two daughters of Shizuto and Hisayo Hanato, Japanese immigrants from Hiroshima. At the outbreak of World War II, the Hanatos ran a small Chinese restaurant in Long Beach. Civilian Exclusion Order #2, issued on March 30, 1942, gave them six days' notice before they were sent to Santa Anita. In early October 1942, the Hanatos boarded a train for Jerome, where their address was 6-4-A. At Jerome, Yoshiko met and married Hideo Endo, a mechanical engineer and the eldest child of Heigoro and Ume Endo of San Pedro. The newlyweds left Jerome for resettlement in Chicago, where they lived until returning to the Los Angeles area in 1952. I was born in Chicago in 1944, grew up in Tujunga, California, and retired in 2008 after a thirty-five-year career as a professor of sociology and Asian American studies at the University of Colorado.

October 20, 1942

Wish we'd gone through Wyoming, Utah, and eight other states to come here, as did the last bunch of arrivals from Santa Anita. From our train window we saw sage brush, odd formations of rocks, and the "lone prairies." . . . The camp arrangement is like all other relocation centers, we're told. Six families occupy one building, and twelve buildings form one block. Each block has its own mess hall, lavatories, and laundry.

September 1975

We had the large end room at Jerome. It had [initially] been assigned to a young couple, the Roy Shibas, with a young child. They had been told that others would be put in with them and asked us to change from a small room, which we did—gladly—and later notified the persons in charge. Our old bedroom carpet

Yoshiko Hanato, Jerome, 1942.

and pink priscilla-type curtains helped furnish the room. Of course, Oba-chan had a flower garden next to our barrack. Fortunately, our block was at the corner of camp—we could see the woods.

October 20, 1942

We constantly see the two to three hundred people in our own block instead of the thousands that we did at Santa Anita, so the atmosphere is more home-like and it's certainly a lot better for the youngsters.... Water here is abundant as well as soft. Only a little soap is necessary for laundry and hardly any scrubbing is needed. Meat, meat, and more meat. Onions, potatoes, and carrots are the only seldom-seen vegetables out this way. And to think we used to complain and crab about the meatless days at Santa Anita.... Yukie [Yoshiko's sister] is at present working as a steno in the engineer's office. I'm helping register the school students, tabulating the subjects they wish to take and so forth in the education department. The number of teachers and curriculum are to be decided from our chart. All jobs are temporary until the camp is filled. The instructors here are very sincere and seem truly interested in the welfare of the children, so the youngsters are fortunate. All the school buildings, church, and store are to be built by the evacuees.... Japanese who have a degree and about fifteen to twenty units in education may be allowed to teach.

December 15, 1942

Your huge box came today . . . at present, we're wondering whether to wait until Christmas . . . or let curiosity take its course. We hear that our Christian friends on the outside are sending gifts to the youngsters here. At our Thanksgiving party, we completely ignored them but since they still believe in Santa Claus, our block is having a social for them this time . . . Even the grownups are yearning for a "white" Christmas. I went with a group of Fresno girls to the fellowship last Sunday, and the Christmas songs were enjoyable. It's so terribly far, church and other activities, and dark that it's practically never that we go out. . . . Getting to be a weatherman now. Didn't feel the rain coming in my rheumatism . . . but I just knew that the last two days of beautiful, typical Southern California weather . . . wasn't going to last. Thunder, rain, and lightning are coming at a furious speed now. Am glad to be indoors by the fire.

December 30, 1942

We were allowed out, a few of us anyway, to Portland—a block-long and one-man-owned town. . . . and had plenty of time to enjoy an ice cream cone and cake. I managed to see from the back of a canvas-covered Army truck because I selfishly grabbed the last seat near the back opening. . . . Nobody gets as sad and low as I do. But you know Miss Sell, I'm coming to believe that beauty is not where you find it but where you look for it . . . it's certainly true in our relationship with each other in such a congested place as this. . . . [My mother] tells me that some people haven't enough [money] to buy warm clothing. . . . The Christmas cards we received are hung across the room—mother's artistic touch. . . . The WRA [War Relocation Authority] is trying to find jobs for the Nisei outside of camp now. Living expenses are high and many localities are antagonistic toward us, so just how many of us can be able to live outside is yet to be seen. . . . The high school texts, about two hundred of them, came in today—and what a job it was stamping and arranging them. . . . Last night as I was dozing off, I heard the sirens of the fire truck come by. Thank heavens it was a false alarm but in that hazy moment of half-sleep and half-awake . . . I thought I was home again, and the engine was racing down Atlantic Ave.

September 1975

Once a friend and I went to a very small town to get refreshments for an education department party. The superintendent let us off and we returned by bus. Wanting to sit together, we sat on the long bench at the rear. The driver stopped, rearranged the other passengers, and asked us to move to the front. Didn't realize until much later that we were sitting in the "colored" section. Probably the first time in my life that I've been considered "white."

April 13, 1943

Our Pop [father] has just returned from a month's sojourn at the center hospital. Our fears of a cerebral hemorrhage or paralysis were fairly groundless to date, but we're not taking any chances. The green foliage on the trees is beautiful and you would love the wild dogwood, violets, wild plum etc. found deep in the woods. Every Sunday we go on a hike or picnic. . . . Of course, there are those annoying snakes and biting mosquitoes. . . . More and more people are being relocated outside and many of my friends have found employment in Chicago and Cleveland. Wish I was trained to do something—then I'd go too.

June 25, 1943

Fellow I've been going with [Hideo Endo] is in Chicago looking for an engineering job. Pop, as usual, has a say-so, so you never can tell.

September 1975

A friend's sister, an optometrist, asked me to try out for receptionist at the optometry clinic. Six optometrists and a waiting list months long. Everybody, but everyone needed glasses. Dr. Kuwahara, from Hilo, was head of the optometry clinic. An extremely jovial man, he'd kid the young Nisei optometrists about being "uptight." He somehow managed to smuggle in liquor, probably from Caucasian employees, for his sukiyaki parties.

June 25, 1943

Our optometrists have all been using their own equipment at the clinic and as their goods depreciated and as the WRA won't replace the worn parts, they have decided to close down here for a while. Some of them are planning to relocate here in the East. As a private practice seems out of the question now, most of them are hoping to work in the larger labs if they can find such work in a city where membership in the CIO is not required. [The optometrists felt, perhaps incorrectly, that the CIO—the Congress of Industrial Organizations union—did not allow Japanese to become members.]

September 18, 1943

A former teacher, now in Colorado, suggested that I write to her friend in Rohwer and have her make arrangements for our wedding in McGehee. No exam of any kind is necessary here, not even a waiting period although the license is $3.60. Mom and I went on a day's shopping trip to Little Rock and bought my going-away suit, hat, and few items for my hope chest.

September 1975

Not wanting to be married by the justice of the peace in a nearby town or in a makeshift camp church, a friend of mine from Hiroshima Jojakuin made arrangements for us to be married at the Presbyterian Church in McGehee. The camp project head, first time I ever saw him, gave me permission to take ten people out [of Jerome] with the promise that "mum's the word." He didn't want others to follow suit.

Looking back forty years later.
Redress Commission testimony, 1981

I strongly believe that the severe medical problems I now have (coronary heart disease, myasthenia gravis, diabetes, arthritis, allergies) had their origin in the camps. The combined stress of bad food, cramped living quarters, the lack of privacy, and the shame and humiliation of being in a concentration camp have taken its toll on my health. . . . My father, a healthy man who had worked sixteen hours a day previous to the internment, developed extremely high blood pressure in camp and after his release was never able to work. Since he received only a pittance in payment for the loss of the new and beautifully decorated restaurant, it was necessary for my mother to work in a cannery to support the family. Nothing can fully compensate for the loss of freedom, but monetary compensation will act as a deterrent and prevent such an act of imprisoning innocent citizens—without due process of law—from happening again.

Rinko Shimasaki Enosaki

I would like to give you a bit of my background. On September 4, 1927, I was born at home in Strathmore, California (five miles from Lindsay) into a family of eight children: Toshimi (Tom), Isao (Ira), Atsuko, Fujio (Fred), Shizuo (Sam), Rinko (me), Wataru (Walter), and Uzuru (Joe). Our family got along well with our white neighbors. My brother, Tom, was the scoutmaster of the local Boy Scout troop. My father, Kurazo Ideta, took care of a vineyard for Mr. Albert Crawford. My father died in 1941 when I was thirteen years old. My mother, Hatsu Shimasaki, worked hard, but came home to cook lunch and supper for the laborers. She was always exhausted and was the first person in bed at night. I loved when it rained, which was rare, because she would read stories in Japanese to us.

Family Number 13850

After the war began with Japan, President Franklin D. Roosevelt issued Executive Order 9066. There were posters of the order displayed in prominent places, telling you how many days you had to close your business. Tom had a strawberry patch and was fortunate to find someone to take care of it, when we were "evacuated" from our home. You were told you could only take what you could carry. That meant two suitcases for me.

Our family was number 13850. I don't know whatever gave me the idea to keep a diary. Most of my entries are the thoughts of a boy-crazy girl, but in some places, I recorded historical facts, like when Hitler died. According to my diary, on May 12, 1942, I said "goodbye" to my friends. Over seventy-five years later, I still keep in contact with one of my former classmates, Naomi Lee Short Ismay.

Fresno Assembly Center

When we arrived at Fresno Assembly Center on May 13, we were in lines for everything. We received typhoid and smallpox vaccinations. Everybody got sick, except my cousin, Miyeko Ideta, who was in the lines, but somehow, she didn't get her immunizations. We stuffed straw into tickings for our mattresses. There were seven of my family in the end barrack. The walls did not go all the way up to the roof, so you could hear what was going on next door. If my memory is correct, we had a group toilet with about six holes to sit on and with water running underneath. When the toilet flushed, whoever was the unfortunate person on the end would get splashed. It was so inconvenient at night to go to the toilet. My mother might have gotten a chamber pot for us to use.

The Shimasaki family—Walt, Sam, Mother Hatsu, Rinko, Joe, and Fred.

On May 16 I met Sachiko Sakaguchi, a Japanese girl who could not speak any Japanese. This was rare for a person of Japanese descent in those days. I don't remember anything else about her, except that she wore a green turban.

At the assembly center, there was a rumor that a white man was married to a Japanese woman. He did not have to go to camp but came to be with her. This is a great love story. We stayed at Fresno Assembly Center until the camps in Arkansas were ready. My brother, Sam, went to Jerome early to help get the camp ready. He got such a bad case of poison ivy that he had to be hospitalized. I recall his infection had an odor, when I visited him after we arrived at Jerome.

Jerome, Arkansas

On October 26, 1942, we left by train to Arkansas and often had to stop to let the troop trains by. We had three meals a day in the dining car with Black waiters. This was the first time I had ever seen a Black person, and this was probably the first time they had seen a Japanese person. When we finally arrived in Arkansas on October 30, the Arkansas residents were expecting to see small people, like me; however, the first person off the train was Dr. Kikuo Taira, a six-foot-tall, robust man. I wrote in my diary that "my address changed to 46-4-E Denson, Arkansas" and "It was terrible because it rained. Muddy. No barracks ready. Ate at the mess hall. No beds, poor drinking water, etc."

Our family again lived in an end barrack. We had a wood-burning stove with trees chopped for firewood. It rained a lot. In order to go to the toilets, showers, and laundry room, we walked on wooden boards to avoid the mud. Our food was okay most of the time. We ate in the mess hall. At first our family ate together, but later the kids wanted to eat with their friends. There was some food I could not eat, like canned squid, hominy, and grits. We were served fish often, which were usually cut in half. There was one little boy who cried if he didn't get the head half, because he loved to eat the eyes! My mother worked in the mess hall washing dishes. She would bring me white rice and *tsukemono* [preserved vegetables] on days I could not eat the food that was served. One time I developed red spots on my thighs, which the doctors thought was due to a lack of vitamin K.

There was a barbed-wire fence around the camp and a guard tower to make sure you did not leave. That's why I call it a concentration camp. It was rumored that a man tried to walk away and was shot. I wish I knew if this was true. My younger brothers, Joe and Walt, wondered what was on the other side of the barbed wire. When the guard walked the other direction, they (and their friends) crawled under the fence and looked around. This was a dangerous thing to do!

The poor Arkansas people living around Jerome resented us being fed and clothed. I would gladly have given them my squid! We received vouchers which we could use to buy basic things at the camp store. We had school in the barracks. Ira had two years of community college education. He taught mechanical drawing. Tom went to Ann Arbor, Michigan, and taught Japanese to the MIS (military intelligence) students. It seemed to me like some white teachers came to camp to just get a job; however, I had a very good teacher, Miss Cash. I graduated high school in camp. I went to church each Sunday. According to my diary, we had a world-renowned evangelist, Dr. E. Stanley Jones, come to speak at Jerome. I asked him for his autograph but have no idea what I did with it. Church people on the outside sent Christmas gifts to the children under sixteen years old. This was very heartwarming.

The Crusaders and the 442nd Regimental Combat Team

My Sunday school teacher was Mary Nakahara (later known as Yuri Kochiyama). After school and in the summer, she organized a group of us to write form letters to the soldiers in the 100th Infantry Battalion and the 442nd Regimental Combat Team, who were serving in Italy and France. We called ourselves the Crusaders.

One of the soldiers wrote to me, "If anything happens to me, remember I fought for girls like you." We sent letters to all the GIs and to generals, too. I think General Mark Clark wrote back to us, thanking us for helping to keep up the morale of the troops. I kept a scrapbook of the letters, and years later I gave the scrapbook to Yuri, who donated it to the Japanese American National Museum in Los Angeles.

The 100th Battalion from Hawaii and the 442nd Regiment from the mainland trained together at Camp Shelby, Mississippi, but there were rivalries between the two groups. Some of the 100th men decided to visit Jerome, because they thought they could get rice and other Japanese food. However, when they arrived at Jerome, they were appalled to see the families of the 442nd men kept behind barbed wire with guards.

The soldiers at Camp Shelby asked the USO from Jerome if they would come entertain them. The older girls who ran the USO said they would come on the condition they could stop along the way to shop. I thought this was such a selfish thing to ask. I was only sixteen years old at the time, but my mother trusted me and said I could go. My younger brothers called me "a Camp Shelby Miss." At Camp Shelby the men took special pains to prepare an elaborate dinner, but I was so excited, I could not eat a thing. It was at Camp Shelby that I met my future husband, George Enosaki. He told me that I was having more fun than anybody else! George had volunteered to serve in the 442nd. His parents, Yoshio and Riwa Enosaki, lived in the barrack next to our family. When he came to visit them, he remembered me from my visit to Camp Shelby, but I didn't remember him at all. We heard that the Germans could not break the code of the 442nd and the 100th because they spoke in Japanese.

Rohwer, Arkansas

After about 1½ years people were allowed to return to their former homes. At that time my family moved from Jerome to Rohwer. (I understood that Jerome was then used for a prisoner of war camp.) People were given travel money to return to California or elsewhere. On January 31, 1945, I went to Chicago to live with Atsuko and worked at the Spiegel catalog company and then the Curtiss Candy Company. At work I could buy a box of twenty-four Baby Ruth candy bars for $2, and it made my mother happy when I brought a box "home" with me, when I returned to Rohwer on June 2. I had returned to help take my mother, who had stomach cancer, to Utah, where my eldest brother, Tom,

Rinko Shimasaki ready to leave camp.

was working. My mother was so ill, she could not walk. On July 26 we left on a special train. When the train reached Salt Lake City on July 28, she was taken off the train on a stretcher through the Pullman window. My mother spent the remainder of her life in a hospital, where Rev. Howard Toriumi, who was fluent in Japanese, visited her every day. After she died on September 23, her body was sent to be buried in Lindsay, California, beside my father. I took my two younger brothers to live with Tom, who looked after them like a father. Then, I traveled back to Chicago to live. When some people returned home, they found their properties ransacked. Our things stored in Tom's bunkhouse were okay.

When I returned to Chicago, I lived with a dear friend, Ruth Hirose, and her sister and brother-in-law, Harry and Lucy Konda. George Enosaki started coming to see me at Harry and Lucy's home. In Chicago when George and I were dating, a couple of women yelled at us, "Go back, you damn dirty Japs!" We got married by Dr. Jitsuo Morikawa on the South Side on August 31, 1946. We had a daughter, Eileen, born at Mother Cabrini Hospital in 1949. George was commuting from Chicago to Gary, Indiana, to his prewar job at Reynolds Metals Plastics Division.

We moved to Gary in 1950 to be closer to his work. There we had a son, Ted, and a daughter, Georgene.

In 1956 when Reynolds Metals moved to Grottoes, Virginia, we moved to Harrisonburg, where I've lived ever since. When we moved to Virginia, it was segregated. We were told not to use the "colored" toilets or entrances. My husband died of a ruptured aneurysm in 1982. I retired at the age of seventy from my job as a case aide for the Social Services Department. In addition to my three children, I now have six grandchildren—Michael Takeo (Tak) Magruder, Richard Matsuo (Mat) Magruder, Kerri Fleming, Heather Fleming, Onna (Kimi) Enosaki Oleson, and Erik Fleming—and three great-granddaughters (Gabrielle Magruder and twins, Saraya and Linaya Oleson). I enjoy every day to the fullest and feel blessed to have lived to ninety-two years old.

Phoebe Ichinaga Grange

My Story

March 25, 1926—I was born in Terra Bella, California, a tiny town in the southern end of the San Joaquin Valley. My first recollection is living in Pixley, California, way out in the country. I remember a water tower adjacent to the house and I remember a cemented "pond" close by. The kitchen had a wood stove.

The next house I remember was when the family moved to Tulare, California, where Father started Jim's Chop Suey restaurant. We moved from that first house to one on N Street, right across the street from the entrance to the Tulare County Fairgrounds. After that, we moved to 449 South M Street. We had a large backyard, but I cannot remember doing any planting—I do remember harvesting tomatoes, green onions, etc. This property is now part of the parking lot for the big trucks from Dairymen's Creamery, which was across the street from our house. This creamery continues business at the same location today. They now make products for Land O'Lakes. At home we all had chores—cleaning house, ironing clothes (Mother always washed the clothes, though), cooking meals, babysitting younger siblings, etc. In my free time I would hang out with my girlfriends, read books from the library, and occasionally allow myself the luxury of a 5¢ cherry Coke from the fountain across the street from Lender's Hardware Store.

At the restaurant, there was a basement that ran the length of the

Reprinted with permission from May Takeda et al., *All We Could Carry: James K. & Kiyono Ichinaga's Children Remember the War Years (1941–46)* (self-pub., Pleasanton, CA: 2004).

Phoebe Ichinaga Grange, 1944.

restaurant and it was down there that Father had a long rectangular table where he made fresh noodles daily. All the kids in the family old enough were put to work there. When Fred and I became old enough, every morning before school we washed dishes, wiped down all the tables, and swept the floor. On weekends we also chopped veggies and cooked down pork skins (from the legs used to make *char sui*), which we sold to the grocery store owned by the Izumis, the only other Japanese family in town. Usually Fred and I split around 80–90¢. I would take my share and deposit it in the Bank of America.

December 7, 1941

I cannot remember where I was on December 7, 1941, or what I was doing. I do not especially remember my parents' reaction. I do remember in the days afterwards I would go to the US Post Office to buy war bonds for Father.

When the evacuation of all Japanese from the West Coast was ordered, barracks were hastily built in the Tulare Fairgrounds where some of the evacuees would be taken until facilities out of state were ready. One of the men who built the barracks was Clark Wicks, a friend of Father's. Our family was not sent to the Tulare facility, but to the Fresno "Assembly Center." I was a sophomore at Tulare High School.

Fresno Assembly Center

I have little recollection of our stay at Fresno. It was hard getting used to being on a strict schedule—especially mealtimes. I recall a couple of occasions when friends of my parents from Tulare drove up to see us. Father had arranged for a friend and his family to live in our house at 449 during our absence.

Jerome, Arkansas

After a short stay in Fresno, we were transported by train to the Jerome Relocation Center in Arkansas. (There was a second center in Arkansas called Rohwer Relocation Center.) There were armed soldiers on the train. Occasionally, the train would stop so the people could get out and stretch. Of course, these stops were always somewhere in the desert—in the middle of nowhere. I can still remember the desolate land traveling through Texas.

Upon our arrival, the family was assigned to barracks. I remember the older siblings lived in the largest room that each barrack contained. The rooms were furnished sparsely. We had army-type cots with mattresses filled with straw.

What was a typical day in Jerome? We attended school, about four to five blocks away. Most of the teachers were fellow evacuees, and most of them had been qualified teachers in California.

However, two of my teachers (one was Miss Cash) were from Arkansas. Miss Cash taught history and geography and the second teacher taught physical education classes (I loved listening to the southern accents). Each block had a mess hall where all three meals each day were served. I assume I ate with the family. In each block there was a building for showers, laundry tubs, and toilets. I made friends through school, neighbors, and church. I had never attended church regularly . before Jerome, but I began attending church and was baptized before we left. The family pretty much settled into a routine. May and Jack obtained jobs—for the grand sum of about $9 a month. I think doctors were paid $19 a month. Father got a job overseeing the running of all the mess halls.

Occasionally there was block dance in the recreation room. We would play waltzes on the record player.

Arkansas weather was a change from Central California. I can remember Arkansas clouds moving across the sky—just racing. Clouds seemed to appear without any warning. After a rain, the heavy clay soil played havoc with shoes and keeping rooms clean was a constant job. The woods surrounding the camp had beautiful wild dogwood trees. The woods also had abundant "flying" squirrels.

While in Jerome, Dorothy left for Scottsbluff, Nebraska, to attend junior college. She was sponsored by a Methodist church family. Later, Jack and May left for Chicago, Illinois, where they had jobs waiting for them. The rest of the family left for Mitchell, Nebraska, sometime in May—right before my graduation from high school. I received my high school diploma from the Jerome Relocation Center. When the family arrived in Mitchell, I reenrolled in the local high school, but only had to take a couple of classes since I had already received my diploma from Jerome.

Father became a sharecropper with a native Nebraskan Japanese family—and it turned out to be a disaster. I moved to Lincoln, Nebraska, where Dorothy was attending the University of Nebraska. I enrolled in a commercial business school, run by Warren Thomas's uncle. I must have paid for at least some of my tuition. I remember being very upset when I was notified I needed to pay $5 before receiving my diploma. I did not send money, but they mailed my diploma anyway. While going to school, I found a part-time job at the YMCA. I roomed with two girls from Puyallup, Washington—also evacuees. I was able to support myself. I remember that occasionally Mother would mail boxes of home-grown veggies. A coworker at the Y (also a part-timer) was Theodore Sorensen, who later became a speechwriter for President John Kennedy.

Lincoln, Nebraska

Lincoln, Nebraska, gave me my first experience with falling snow. I remember walking back to my apartment from work when it started to snow, and I was amazed that there was absolutely no sound as the snowflakes hit the ground. I do not know what my expectations were. Do you want to know what song was popular that year? It was "Don't Fence Me In" and I can still remember humming this song as I walked home in the snow. During this time there was rationing of certain food items, etc. I can remember especially rationing of sugar, meat, gasoline, etc. We ate a lot of Spam.

After the ban was lifted that prevented the Japanese from returning to the West Coast, the family moved back to California. However, May and I stayed a while longer since there wasn't room in the cars for us, and we took the train back to Tulare while Dorothy returned to Lincoln. Once I got back, I found a job as a secretary in the Department of Unemployment on M Street.

Phoebe Ichinaga Grange, 2004.

It is amazing that my parents were able to cope with this whole experience as they did, and it is to their credit that all their children turned out to be law-abiding, tax-paying citizens. Needless to say, I am proud to be their daughter.

Anna Sakaizawa Hasegawa

I was moved by Lily's [Lily Imahara Metz's] remembrances in this volume; my only wish was that my ninety-two-year-old brain would dig down and pull out some comparable memories. We'll just do the best we can.

Many of the physical details in Lily's memories match mine. Our age differences and particular family situations, I'm sure, led to differences in internalized experiences. For example, being a fourteen-year-old teenager, the whole internment camp experience felt not too different from the experience of attending a summer youth camp, including rules and restrictions. Even the physical accommodations had some similarity!

Best of all, there were lots of other teenagers around—all Japanese American! What an experience . . . in a short time we were attending social activities together, making friends, organizing sports, musical and craft offerings, eventually attending school. For us teenagers, it was a time of social opportunity.

For our parents and other adults, on the other hand, we teenagers were somewhat aware that life was something else—a time of real crises. They were losing businesses, property, financial investments, important relationships, etc. I honor my parents for never having "put down" the United States to us, instead assuring us that things would eventually turn out all right. My father had great confidence in the US Constitution, having fled Japan's growing militarism as a teenager and having received a college education through Quaker benefactors.

(A side story: My father was picked up by the FBI and put into a political prison immediately after Pearl Harbor. He was released in time to go to Jerome, Arkansas, from the Santa Anita Assembly Center in California. After Jerome was closed, our family was sent to Camp Amache in Colorado [the Granada Relocation Center]. As the war was ending, the Navy hired my father to help with the interpretation in the peace process. We understood, but were not sure of details. Just the irony.)

You asked if I graduated from Jerome High School. Yes, I'm enclosing a photograph of my brother, Johnny, and myself. We were just 1½ years apart and when we moved from one city to another in the middle of a school year (my father was a Japanese schoolteacher), I was put up a half grade and my brother was put down a grade, so we ended in class together, poor Johnny. I'm remembering one interesting incident from high school. It must have been in social studies class. Somehow the subject of southern racial discrimination came up. I think the teacher had made some statement about volunteering to come into the camp from the "outside" to teach in our school because she felt we were being unfairly detained . . . I wish I could clearly remember the details! But some of the boys jumped on her and pressed her about the treatment of Blacks in the South. I only recall—she backed off and kept saying, "But you folks don't understand." We can wonder if her awareness changed any in the following years.

Anna and Johnny.

Please understand, I do not wish to imply the segregation was all fun and games. However, I think dwelling on physical aspects misses the point. After all, we were not beaten and starved as were the Jews in Germany. When asked to speak about my experience, I always stress that justice was the issue. Taking away the freedom and constitutional rights of human beings without just cause is immoral—always wrong! Furthermore, we are all appointed to the task of stepping forward and speaking out when we see others put in similar endangered situations.

ANNA SAKAIZAWA HASEGAWA

Janet Yomogida Hayashi

This is a short summary of my life. My name is Janet Yomogida Hayashi. I am the third child of George and Ruth Yomogida, born in October 1933 in Long Beach, California. We originally lived on the west side of Long Beach and in 1939, my parents built their home at 1857 Locust Avenue. At that time, I lived there with my two sisters, Evelyn Yomogida Matoi and Joanne Yomogida Okada, and our brother Herb. We had a very happy and normal childhood attending local schools and were members of the Japanese Grace Presbyterian Church. Our bubble burst when the war broke out in 1941.

After December 7, 1941

In 1942, because of our Japanese ancestry, we were ordered by the government to evacuate our home in Long Beach. There were one hundred twenty thousand Japanese American citizens on the West Coast who were affected. We had three days to pack our clothes and essentials. We were allowed only one bag per person. My parents lost all their possessions. My dad lost his very successful produce business, his trucks, and a car. Even at my young age of eight, I remember being so frightened and confused and could not understand why we were so abruptly uprooted from our home.

Santa Anita Assembly Center

We were sent to Santa Anita racetrack, a so-called assembly center. They housed us in the horse stables. It was impossible to get rid of the terrible stench no matter how much we cleaned. My family of six slept in one horse stable. We were provided with cots, which we filled with hay to make them more comfortable to sleep on. We had no running water. We

Janet (top row, far left) doing the hula dance, Rohwer, Arkansas, 1943.

Janet (top row, third from right, in the dark skirt) twirling baton, Rohwer, Arkansas, 1943.

had to go to another building to use the bathroom and shower facilities. Somehow, we endured these deplorable living conditions for six months.

Jerome and Rohwer War Relocation Centers

From Santa Anita we were sent to Jerome and then to Rohwer, Arkansas. The newly constructed barracks were built for us. The conditions were not much better but at least they were clean. Coming from nice California weather, we had to get acclimated to the Arkansas weather. The summers were blazing hot and the winters were freezing cold. The men and women had their separate restrooms and shower facilities. One lady hung sheets over the stalls so we could have some privacy. Japanese people are very innovative. The women made *tsukemono* [preserved vegetables] with watermelon rinds and green tops of radishes, so we always had plenty of

JANET YOMOGIDA HAYASHI

tsukemono and *gohan* [rice topped with egg]. We all ate our meals in one large mess hall. My father was in charge of cooking the rice and made $19 a month.

Because I was so young, my life in camp was more or less carefree. We were provided with regular classrooms so we could continue our education. I learned to do the hula dance and twirl the baton. We were invited to provide some entertainment at different functions. I am sure my parents were very concerned and worried about what the future held for us. I do remember being guarded day and night by soldiers carrying rifles in their guard towers and being BEHIND BARBED-WIRE fences twenty-four hours a day. My parents never lost their faith in God and always told us to *gaman* [persevere] and stay strong and everything will be all right. I later met my future husband, Jim Hayashi, when his family relocated to Long Beach. They originally resided in Salinas, California, when they were ordered to evacuate to the Poston Relocation Center in Arizona. They were incarcerated there for the duration of the war.

Congressional Medal of Honor

My husband Jim Hayashi's cousin, S.Sgt. Joe Hayashi, who served with the 442nd unit, was awarded posthumously the Congressional Medal of Honor, the nation's highest decoration, for his heroism and bravery. Joe saved many of his comrades while sacrificing his own life when their unit came under attack in Tendola, Italy. Joe's sister, Chiye Watanabe, was presented the decoration by President Bill Clinton on June 21, 2000, at the White House. How ironic that while Joe was serving with the 442nd Combat Team, the highly distinguished and most decorated unit, he came to visit his family who were still incarcerated in Camp Poston, Arizona. After visiting his family, Joe returned to his

Memorial listing Medal of Honor recipients at the Go For Broke Monument in Los Angeles, California. *Photo: Walter Imahara.*

army unit. It was soon after that Joe was sent overseas. It was while fighting the Germans in Italy that he lost his life. That was the last time his family saw him alive. Joe's father (Chukichi) and Jim's father (Ihei) were brothers.

Long Beach, California

The war was over in August 1945. After four years of being incarcerated, we were released to return to our homes. We were one of the few families who had a home to return to because my mother was told if she paid the property taxes, they could not sell our home. Somehow, she was able to make the payments. My father started his gardening business and soon had many customers. That is how he supported us. By that time, there were eight of us in the family. My brother Glenn was born in camp in Arkansas and my brother Harold was born in Long Beach after we returned from camp. After the family got settled, our lives returned to normal. I attended Washington Junior High School and graduated from Long Beach Poly High School in 1951. That's when life started getting better for me and the family.

I would be very remiss if I didn't acknowledge my parents, George and Ruth Yomogida. When we returned from Arkansas, many families had lost their homes and possessions when they were so abruptly evacuated. My parents helped many families get back on their feet by providing hot meals and a place to stay. They encouraged their friends to keep faith and everything will be fine. Their friends were forever grateful for their generosity and help.

I will be forever grateful to my parents who had so much courage and stayed strong after enduring so many hardships. My father, George, lived to be 88 years old and my mother, Ruth, lived to the ripe old age of 102.

David Ichinaga

I was born in Sidney, Nebraska, in October 1945. World War II had just ended, and I have no personal experiences of those years that my brothers and sisters had. What I do have are the stories that my father and mother related to me when the subject of our family's incarceration was brought up. These stories would come up from time to time because of some incident but would never be related or told to me when I asked questions specifically about the war.

Fresno, California

Because of Pop's food experience he was asked to help prepare food for all of the internees, and for that he was considered a traitor by the older Japanese in the Fresno camp to the degree that they thought that Pop was putting or going to put poison in their food. He was very proud that he was asked to assist with the evacuation and made it a point that I understood that our family was one of the very last to leave the Fresno camp and California by train to Jerome, Arkansas.

Jerome, Arkansas

Pop's sergeant in charge of a mess hall asked Pop if he would like to accompany him into town to buy some supplies. Not only did Pop agree but [he] asked his sergeant if he could stop for a beer. Pop was dropped off in front of a local bar and he walked in, sat down, and ordered a beer from

Reprinted with permission from May Takeda et al., *All We Could Carry: James K. & Kiyono Ichinaga's Children Remember the War Years (1941–46)* (self-pub., Pleasanton, CA: 2004).

David Ichinaga,
1948.

the bartender. Sitting across on the other side of the bar were two locals having beers. One of the other locals drinking beer yelled at Pop and said, "Hey, boy, what the hell are you doing! Pick up your beer, go outside and sit over here now!" Pop, fearing for his life because he believed that it was because he was Japanese, moved quickly to avoid any confrontation. As Pop walked out the door, he saw on that the side of the bar that he had entered was a sign for COLORED PEOPLE ONLY. Once inside the white-only side of the bar, one of the locals replied, "That's better, boy." Pop's first experience of racism in the South.

A Black soldier had his feet tied by chains and was pulled behind a Jeep until dead and then dropped off in front of the barracks of one of the Japanese families. He was accused of raping a Japanese girl.

After the war, Pop had charge of prisoners that were German and Italian. He treated them with respect and made sure that they got plenty of food daily. They thanked him and gave him a vinegar bottle hand-painted with a model sailing ship inside, made out of wooden matches and hand-carved wood.

David Ichinaga,
2003. *Photo:*
Norman
Yamauchi.

Sidney, Nebraska

A picture of Pop, Sock Yamashita, and his other buddies standing inside the Sioux Ordnance Depot with shotguns and hundreds of pheasants they had just shot. There was a barbed-wire fence with guard tower in the background and a sign that said, "Any trespassers will be shot on sight." Mom said that she would cook up the pheasants and put them in Mason jars to be given out to friends.

Tulare, California

I had just received my hunting license and asked Pop if I could buy my first shotgun! His response was for us to get in the car and drive to the Eastside of Tulare. We stopped in front of a house and Pop instructed me to knock on the door and let the guy inside know that I was Jim Ichinaga's son and that I wanted one of his shotguns. The guy responded that he didn't have any of Pop's shotguns and didn't know what I was talking about. I returned to the car and relayed the message to Pop and he immediately returned to the house. After a few minutes he had three of his guns back, with which I still hunt today. These guns were given to the guy in Tulare to safeguard until Pop's return from camp . . . this is the same guy that Mom and Pop trusted to live in our house in Tulare during the war for free rent. The story relayed to me was that not only did they return to a dirty house, but also Pop's fish pond outside the kitchen window was destroyed by this same individual.

Again, I want to state that Pop and Mom would never answer any questions about their incarceration during the war to me and that these stories were told to me only as a byproduct of some other incident or story.

Jack Ichinaga

In the fall of 1941, I was nineteen years old, attending classes at College of the Sequoias in Visalia, and working at Jim's Chop Suey. Beginning my freshman year in high school, my duties included making all the noodles for the restaurant. I got up around 4:00 a.m. and made the noodles and cleaned the place before I went to school. Lunchtime I came back to help in the kitchen and worked until about 8:00 p.m. washing dishes, pots, and pans. If it was busy, I also boiled the noodles. On the very few days Mom and Dad would take a day off to go to Pismo Beach, my sister May and I were responsible for working the restaurant. Those were stressful days as then I did all the cooking while May did the waitressing. I could never get the food out fast enough for May. We were always relieved when Mom and Pop would waltz in the door at around 7:00 p.m. to take over.

We listened to a lot of music at the restaurant. We had a jukebox with 78 rpm records that were about a fourth-inch thick. I believe it cost a nickel to play. We bought every new record. The jukebox paid for the gas and the electric bill. I didn't have a lot of free time, but when I did, I was active—playing basketball and baseball, fishing, hunting, going to the movies. Pop paid me $5 per week and I spent most of my money on clothes and fun. Uncle John sold me his Model A for $200. Eventually I started saving by paying monthly premiums on a life insurance policy with New York Life.

On December 7, 1941, I attended services at the Baptist church with George Katsuki. Later someone in church said President Roosevelt

Reprinted with permission from May Takeda et al., *All We Could Carry: James K. & Kiyono Ichinaga's Children Remember the War Years (1941–46)* (self-pub., Pleasanton, CA: 2004).

announced that Pearl Harbor was bombed and there were a lot of casualties. George and I took off for the restaurant as soon as we heard the news. My dad's first reaction was that he had to get a birth certificate. There was no problem with the customers.

Jack Ichinaga, 1944.

Shortly after the Pearl Harbor attack, there was an order in California that persons of Japanese descent needed a special permit if they traveled more than five miles out of the town and they had to be home by 8:00 p.m. Since the mayor of Tulare, Monte Williams, was a good friend of Dad's, we had permission to come and go when we opened or closed the restaurant. I was nineteen at the time, so if they wanted to arrest me—so what? I had my birth certificate and carried it with me in case I was stopped.

Being over eighteen, I had to register for the draft. When I received my card, I was classified as 4C, an enemy alien. Shortly after the Pearl Harbor attack, a friend and I drove to Fresno to enlist in the Navy. We were both refused. After that, I was no longer interested in serving in the armed forces.

In April 1942, Japanese Americans from Ventura County started being sent to the Tulare County Fairgrounds (just one long block from our house! It was later called the Tulare Assembly Center). The internees used to come to the fence near the gate and ask if we could buy them brooms and mops and buckets. The guards were very friendly, and we were permitted to purchase the items they requested.

By April 1942, it was clear that we would be sent somewhere. After conferring with Dad, we decided to close the restaurant. I quit junior college so I could help. The booths and the big equipment were stored in Mr. Foster's barn, near the Uchidas' home. We removed most of the hardware and fixtures. We finished moving nearly everything, and the first week in May we were given orders to leave Tulare in the second week in May. We built a lean-to to store the cars, but at the last minute Dad sold the new Pontiac. We just stored the Model A. We had a few fixtures we stored in the garage and used the upper rooms to store furniture and dry-food supplies from the restaurant. We let Mr. Earles live rent-free to take care of our property.

Our family left for Fresno Assembly Center with only the baggage we could carry. We had to go to the American Legion Hall about four blocks from home to be transported there. I got a job as a stock clerk at $8 a month. They made a newsreel showing the camp and to top it off they had the nerve to put white linen on the tables with food that they took away after filming the documentary. I continued to send my premiums in for my life insurance policy. One day I received a letter from New York Life saying they were dropping my policy because I wasn't a US citizen. I sent a copy of my birth certificate along with my premium, but they returned both.

The Fresno Assembly Center was just a temporary place for the internees. Once the actual camps were constructed, the families were sent to the various camps. My warehouse gang stayed behind and took inventory of all the goods as they were returned to the warehouse. We were the last people to leave the Fresno Assembly Center and in December our crew went to Jerome Relocation [Center] in Arkansas.

My warehouse gang was originally supposed to have jobs waiting for us in Jerome, but all the jobs were filled. We finally talked to the head of the administration and got the jobs as head of supplies in different departments, which paid a whopping $12 a month. The doctors and heads of departments received $19 a month. As head of the blanket and bedding supplies, I was supposed to keep an inventory of what came in and what went out. Well, when the last of the camp was filled, it was people from Hawaii. Most of them were wearing zoris [Japanese-style flip-flops], no shoes, no heavy sweaters, so I felt sorry for them. I told the admittance office that I was going to give them extra blankets, etc. and I got the okay. Oh, it was raining sheets of ice; can you imagine how cold it was for them to relocate in this part of the country?

In early 1943, I was given the options of joining the armed services or leaving camp to work in the city. Given my prior experiences, I chose the latter. In April I received word that I could relocate to Chicago for a job at Shotwell Candy Manufacturing. I stayed at the YMCA until a bunch of us rented an apartment. At Shotwell, I helped stack and strap the various boxes of candy. It was piecework and for stuff like jellybeans and marshmallows, I was paid 35 cents for each box I stacked. Eventually I started working with the boxes of dehydrated eggs. The assembly teams liked me because I was a fast worker. Eventually my weekly pay was over $100 for only 40 hours of work per week. I didn't see my apartment mates very often as we all worked in different areas and on different shifts. We did manage to have fun. I spent a lot of time bowling and carousing. I worked at Shotwell Candy Manufacturing until Dad wrote me telling me to rejoin the family in Mitchell, Nebraska.

When Dad moved the family to Mitchell, they moved to a church property with the kitchen upstairs. I came later and slept downstairs. We didn't stay there too long because some people in town put up a burning cross. From there we stayed with the Yamadas, the family we were share-cropping with. I don't remember if it was a chicken coop or a cow shed. We did sharecrop onions, cabbage, celery, tomatoes, and potatoes. During the winter we sorted potatoes and placed them in hundred-pound sacks and put them in the railroad car for shipment. Hail hit our crops twice, so our production was down. I worked with Dad in the potato cellar until we (including May) got a job at Sioux Ordnance Depot in Sidney, Nebraska.

Later, we moved to Sidney Ordnance Depot where the army trans-ferred ammunition into storage facilities called igloos. The family was doing okay, and I hated the cold Nebraskan winter, so I returned to Chicago.

When I was hired at the TraveLite Trailer Company they had five persons on this one job. I said that it probably only takes two, so they said that they would go along and give us so much per the flooring and so much for the sides. Since they needed more help, they were willing to try my suggestion. On my own I bought an angle iron and jigged the flooring, so they were at the same place for the supports and the two sides. The five people they had could not make two a day, but with the two of us with the jig we exceeded three a day and did other piecework jobs. They said, hey, those guys are making too much money, so they planned to cut our piecework rate. I took off the angle iron and quit since we knew that they needed us to increase their production. Yup, they relented and had us come back with more pay. I worked there until I was inducted into the US Army.

I entered the service at Fort Sheridan, Illinois. I was later sent to Camp Polk, Louisiana, for basic training, then to Brooks General for medical training. Then they sent me to Camp Stoneman, California, to the Philippines, then to Okinawa as a dispensary clerk until I got discharged at Fort Lewis, Washington.

Jack Ichinaga, 2000.

I continued to pursue New York Life for reinstatement of my life insurance policy. They continued to refuse me despite being a citizen and a veteran. Later on when I was working for McDonnell Douglas in Los Angeles, the human resources people told me to waive my claim with the insurance company or my job would be terminated. I signed the waiver and received an insurance policy, which ran out in 1960 (I'm still alive so I never collected a penny).

James Ichinaga

When the Japanese struck Pearl Harbor, Hawaii, on December 7, 1941, I was eleven years old and in the sixth grade at Wilson Elementary School in Tulare, California. I loved sports and the perks of being the son of prominent business parents. My earliest recollection was that of living in a small house on South L Street in Tulare. We moved later to a larger two-story house on South M Street to accommodate a larger family. We lived in that house until our forced "evacuation" in May 1942.

Perhaps because I was a middle child, I became the rascal of the family and found it was difficult to conform to the quiet ways of my siblings. I suppose I was considered to be the "black sheep" of our family. I believe I was the first in the family to come home with tattered clothes because of the fight I had with one of my young classmates. Mom nearly fainted and was horrified that one of her sons did battle at such an early age. The fight happened because of taunts that a bully inflicted upon me and, by gosh, I wasn't going to put up with it. I don't know where I got this trait; perhaps it is the stubbornness that runs in our family.

Our chores were automatically given to us by our parents to be a part of their restaurant business. As we became older our responsibilities increased. My job at the age of eight was to collect all empty beverage bottles consumed the night before and to put them in their respective empty cases. My other duties were to sweep the floor and clean the messy booths that had been used the previous night.

On Sunday, December 7, 1941, I was at the Tulare Bowl on J Street with my friends bowling a few games. I remember being frightened because suddenly the news came that the Japanese had attacked Pearl

Reprinted with permission from May Takeda et al., *All We Could Carry: James K. & Kiyono Ichinaga's Children Remember the War Years (1941–46)* (self-pub., Pleasanton, CA: 2004).

Harbor; I no longer was a kid bowling with his friends, I became Japanese to those around me. I biked back to the restaurant to get Pop's view of the situation and on what might become of us.

Jim Ichinaga, 1944.

So much happened and was happening those ensuing months before internment and are now a blur. The government imposed a curfew on our family. We were not to be out after 8 p.m. They allowed us to conduct business as usual, but we had to have the authorities escort our family home when we closed the restaurant each night. We were restricted to a five-mile radius while waiting for our pending evacuation.

During these early days of the war, paranoia set in; Tulare had air-raid test practices. We had to use blackout curtains to cover the windows at night in case the enemy would want to bomb our town. In retrospect it sounds ridiculous and laughable that the enemy would target our town of Tulare. What would the enemy accomplish, kill a lot of cows? Tulare was a small farm town about halfway between Los Angeles and San Francisco with a population of about 9,500.

Before our evacuation to the Fresno Assembly Center, our own Tulare Fairgrounds became the Tulare Assembly Center for the Japanese Americans from the Los Angeles area. I never could understand why they sent us fifty miles north when we could have walked to the Tulare camp one block from our house. I remember riding my bike with some of my friends to check out the "enemies" being bussed into the Tulare camp. There was barbed wire strung along the fences to keep the so-called enemy confined to that area. There were manned, armed sentry towers, so none could escape. How ironic it was that these people looked like me, were innocent like me, but were standing on the opposite side of the fence from me. But our own time to leave was shortly after that when we were ordered to get on a bus that would take us to the Fresno Assembly Center in Fresno, California, where we would begin our prison life.

May 13, 1942, was the last day we saw Tulare until about four years later when we were allowed to return home. This was a black day for us. I remember seeing my father cry for the first time ever and it frightened me because he was our "rock." Questions abounded in our minds. . . . Where are they taking us? What will become of us? How could "our" government take us from the only life I had known? What awaited us at our destination? Yes, the unknown scared me. What lurked in the shadows in the black days ahead?

We were told that we could bring all the baggage we wanted. The only catch was that it was only what we could carry. The essential items obviously were clothing and shoes, but sister Dorothy felt she needed the old portable Remington typewriter with a large "I" painted on the carrying case. I wonder whatever became of that typewriter.

Fresno Assembly Center was a hastily built camp at the Fresno County Fairgrounds. The area of the camp that our barracks were built upon was originally the horse stalls in the fairground area. The barrack that was assigned to us was more like a rectangular-shaped shed that was sectioned off with walls between the rooms. The outer wall was constructed with rough lumber and was covered with tar paper that might protect the building from the rain. I think the roof was made of the same material, too. Asphalt was our floor covering. It got sticky during the hot summer months. There was no ceiling; you could look up and see the rafters that supported the roof. If you have ever been in Fresno during the summer, you would know how hot it becomes, especially in black-colored buildings during the day. The Fresno nights were no bargain, either. Some nights were so stifling it was hard to breathe. We were issued mattresses that we were to fill with straw and the blankets were khaki colored, army issue. Dust was everywhere. It was impossible to escape it. Privacy was nonexistent. Our voices had to be muffled so our neighbors would not be offended.

The first week was dedicated to getting a whole series of vaccinations —typhoid, smallpox, and others for general health reasons. Many of us became sick from the shot itself as the serum was made from the virus they were protecting us against.

"When you get lemons, make lemonade." It is natural for humans to make the best of it at trying times. I will say this for the newly gathered prisoners: they were very resourceful in using what was available to them in a bad situation. They took advantage of the scrap lumber that was surplus from the hastily built buildings. They were very innovative in making useful items to make their lives more bearable and convenient. Lumber was a very precious commodity in those early days of camp. The men built benches, bookshelves, tables, windmills, and wooden clogs called *geta* from the scrap material.

The detainees (prisoners) were very organized during these early times of camp life. I don't know if it was a job that was given to them or if they were just especially innovative organizing different special events for entertainment. I can't recall if we were allowed to have radios. Of course, in the 1940s there were no TV sets. Radio and the newspaper was our method of getting information from the country and the world. Our camp newspaper's name was the *Fresno Grapevine*. It was published two or three times a month. I believe that the population of our Fresno camp peaked to around 5,500 evacuees and there were more children than adults.

The detainees pooled their talents to produce all kinds of shows: art shows, flower arranging, sumo and judo contests, baseball games, and various talent shows on the weekend evenings. These talent shows featured the camp's singers, comedians, magic performers, jugglers, and musicians. Those evenings took away some of the bitterness and anxiety of being incarcerated.

Jerome, Arkansas

I don't know how long we stayed in Fresno, but if I were to guess I would say about six months. If that is correct, then I would say we were put on a train that delivered us to a little burg called Denson, Arkansas, sometime during the month of October or November of 1942. The concentration camp (they were called relocation camps) was given the name Jerome because it is the closest town nearby.

The train ride was lengthy. Many of us became ill because of the heat and confinement of that peculiar rail trip. Our train ride from Fresno to beyond the California border was ordered done with all the shades pulled down for security reasons. (Security reasons?) These were our homes and farmlands that were being blocked from our sight. These were farmlands that many of these train riders had grown their crops upon. The largest town that we passed by was Bakersfield. This city was not really a particularly strategic area in California.

I remember our train being "side railed" many times so that other trains that had priority could pass. During some of these brief times, we were allowed to get off the train to stretch our legs, whoop, and holler. Our train was guarded by soldiers armed with rifles and affixed bayonets.

I have often wondered what the armed guards' orders were in case someone would be foolish enough to try to escape. Would they have shot to kill? There are no records of anyone trying to escape. But then, why would we want to escape? There was no place that we wanted to be except back home.

Jerome, Arkansas, is a little blip on the map, about twelve miles west of the Mississippi River, which borders the state of Mississippi. It is about thirty miles north of the state of Louisiana. The town we lived in was called Denson, about one mile north of Jerome. If you looked at a map today, you wouldn't find Denson [the official post-office designation for the Jerome camp].

If I were ever in charge of punishing a group of people, this is the place I would send them. The environmental elements were very hostile. It was hot and humid in the summer, freezing in the winter. Insects and snakes were the primary inhabitants of this wooded and swampy area. The Jerome camp was surrounded by a barbed-wire fence, as was the Fresno Center. There were sentry towers about every hundred yards or so, occupied by armed soldiers. The woods, swamps, and creeks were inhabited with water moccasins and copperheads and rattlesnakes. I remember seeing those odd creatures called flying squirrels, bats, many species of birds, those wonderful insects called fireflies, and hearing the noisy croaking of the frogs at night. To this day I have never seen mosquitoes as huge as those in Arkansas.

Dad got the prestigious job of steward of all the camp's mess halls, procuring food locally. The government allowed him special permission to leave camp. His job was to ensure that the food supply was ample for the forty-six mess halls that served food for all the prisoners. He had held a similar job in the Fresno Center, but this entailed feeding more people. For this responsibility, he was paid $19 a month, which was the top pay scale in our camp.

Our living quarters once again were in the barrack-style buildings that we had in the Fresno Center, but they were built much better. The partitions between the rooms went to the ceiling and offered better sound protection. But trying to squeeze twelve members of our family into three rooms tested our patience. We found it was lucky for us that we at least liked each other! The heating system consisted of a potbelly stove that used coal and chopped wood as fuel. I for one had never seen a stove like that and I'm sure none of us had ever seen what coal looked like. The dirty smudge of the emissions from burning coal leaves a dingy film on everything and the smell is one we won't soon forget. I remember when the Japanese from Hawaii came to our camp. They were puzzled when they tried to light the stove. They would quickly put a match to the coal and then quickly jump back as if it would suddenly burst into flames.

The first month of camp life brought on new challenges. There was a shortage of firewood and the men would go into the forest to cut trees and haul it back using mules and wagons. I can still visualize "pairs" of our block's residents sawing wood with huge saws that had handles on both ends.

All the men, women, and children had to adjust to their new lifestyle. They soon became restless with the life that was imposed upon them. They were not accustomed to all the leisure hours that their new life gave them. In the past many had worked from dawn to dusk in order to survive and provide extra comforts for their families. Most of the families were farmers who knew only grueling work in the fields.

Many of the women enrolled in all kinds of classes, learned new crafts (such as knitting and crochet), and many, for the first time, were able to take English lessons. I remember Mom knitting woolen caps and slippers for us. The harsh winter in Jerome demanded it. The Sears, Roebuck and Montgomery Ward catalogs were coveted and important reading material for them. We called these catalogs "wish books." Woolen yarns and clothing were ordered from these tattered catalog pages. These catalog companies received a huge amount of business from all ten relocation camps.

The men had to find new hobbies to fill in their leisure time because they no longer could fish and hunt. Cameras and guns were not permitted. Our father joined many other men in our camp who scoured the forest for gnarled, knotted pieces of trees and roots from the many oak, cypress, hickory, and persimmon trees that grew in that area. They would cut these strange-looking pieces, peel the bark off, rub them mirror smooth, and put a coat of shellac on them.

The Japanese "coined" these art objects *kobu*, which translates in English as "bump on the head" or "knot head." I remember that those beautiful pieces of Dad's hung on our walls and were displayed on our mantels for decades.

Things became bearable as we quickly adjusted to the routine of our new lifestyle even though we were still denied our constitutional rights.

Church services of all faiths were held, schools attended, babies were born, the sick and old died, we lived from day to day. I was quite relieved to find this probably would be the worst punishment we might receive, for having the faces of the "enemy."

Sixty years have passed since the start of our incarceration and I am amazed that we never discussed the camp food of that period. The inmates were our cooks and food handlers as well as the dishwashers and cleanup crew. Our family discovered meals that we had only heard of before. We were introduced to corned beef hash, hominy, chicken à la King on toast, lamb curry, macaroni and cheese, shredded wheat, cream of wheat, and a slew of other strange concoctions. This new adventure in "gourmet" food like wieners and sauerkraut took us to new levels. And how about Spam cooked in a variety of ways? Magnificent!

I remember when "Our Government" started giving our young men "loyalty oaths" and how quickly these young men were drafted into the military service. I remember some of these young soldiers, after boot camp, returning to camp to visit their parents in "Our Concentration Camps." They were ordered overseas to fight for America while their parents were in "Our Concentration Camps." I remember the parents of these soldiers displaying the "Blue Stars" in their barrack windows proudly, signifying that their sons were serving "Our Country." Many of these young Japanese American soldiers never made it back to the US; they were buried overseas while their parents were confined.

I am not positive when "Our Government" realized the folly of their decision to incarcerate the law-abiding Japanese, especially since about 70 percent were citizens. There were vocal outbursts of criticism of the mistakes the WRA was making because of the cost—and as an afterthought, the constitutional reasons—however, there were still the clamors of zealots who wanted us shipped back to Japan. About a year after intelligence studies revealed that we were not a threat to society (was that any surprise?), our Army security guards began to be assigned to more important duties. The WRA began searching for cities outside of the West Coast that would hire the eligible working-age detainees. At that time, we were still restricted from living on the West Coast of America.

It is impossible to forget the hardships that our parents endured during these rough times. This fact will always be with us. My siblings would agree with me that the damage done to our parents and thousands of more parents can never be forgotten or repaid by words or monetary means. Many had died before "monetary reparations" were finally paid by our government. Dad was one of these unfortunate ones. He deserved it more than the rest of us. Many of the parents who did receive the "reparations" were too old to really enjoy their use. It is futile to dwell on this matter because nothing can be done about it, yet it is impossible to forget.

James Ichinaga, 2003. *Photo: Norman Yamauchi.*

I truly believe that the human psyche tries to forget and forgive more than it tries to keep bitterness locked inside. We must explain to our children the injustice and humiliation that transpired so long ago, then let it go and permit the healing process to take its natural course.

However, we must always remember that we must be vocal about the injustice we see around us. We know from experience that our government does not always do the "right" thing.

Monty Ichinaga

Monty's Biographical Notes 1937–1946

Born in Tulare, California, on January 4, 1937, in a white two-story house at 449 South M Street. My father's name was James Kanekichi Ichinaga. My mother's name was Kiyono (Nakano) Ichinaga. At my birth they were thirty-nine and thirty-five years old, respectively. I am the tenth of their thirteen children. My parents owned and operated Jim's Chop Suey restaurant on the south side of Kern Street in Tulare from about 1935 to 1942. At the time they owned two houses on M Street and had a new car. All the older kids worked at the restaurant.

The late 1930s were a time when the United States was trying to recover from the Great Depression. Model A Fords were popular cars—our family owned one. Television had not been developed, so listening to the radio was a favorite pastime. We listened to sports, music, and comedy and mystery programs.

At the advanced age of two years, I decided to walk without going through the crawling stage. Because they had been carrying me for a long time, the family was justifiably worried. It must have been that I learned to be "street" wise at an early age. My father used to subscribe to Japanese . newspapers and when he knew that Japan was going to enter the war, he canceled his subscription.

Just before our evacuation, my father provided some translation services at the Tulare Assembly Center, which was in the Tulare County

Reprinted with permission from May Takeda et al., *All We Could Carry: James K. & Kiyono Ichinaga's Children Remember the War Years (1941–46)* (self-pub., Pleasanton, CA: 2004).

Fairgrounds. At the time of evacuation from Tulare, May 1942, World War II was in progress with both Germany and now Japan. Our family was sent to Fresno Assembly Center, in which we were housed in converted horse stalls. I don't have any memories of life there. But there is a book, *We the People* by Mary Tsukamoto, that describes life both in the Fresno Assembly Center and Jerome Relocation Center.

Monty Ichinaga, 1943.

In October 1942, when the Jerome/Denson (Arkansas) relocation center was completed, we traveled by train. The train would periodically stop, and we were allowed to get out and run around. During one of these stops, I ran under a swing with a wooden seat and got hit in the head.

My first visions of Jerome seem to be the clearing and killing of the many snakes, using the Y's of tree limbs.

I remember one man named Fred Yoshikawa, who later was a successful baseball coach in the Fresno area. He made kites for me from bamboo and paper, and we flew them on the ends of two large spools of thread, so that the kite was just a dot in the sky. He gave me used baseballs and a glove.

I don't remember anything about any elementary school classes I attended at Jerome. I remember that we had a couple of "Tall" books— one was *The Little Engine That Could* and the other was *Mother Goose Rhymes*. To remember that, I must have read those books over and over.

I don't remember much about our barracks. Our barracks had coal stoves for cooking. Our beds must have been army bunk bed types.

I do remember that my first experience in playing with matches, with some other boys, occurred behind one of the barracks. It was mainly lighting matches and putting them out. Luckily no damage occurred.

I got mumps twice during our stay in Jerome. I also remember my arms being tied to the bed at night when I got a bad case of poison ivy. I remember the mustard packs for our colds and solutions for constipation. Mustard packs were sheets of newspaper that were coated with some type of mustard. These mustard-coated sheets were then applied to our chest or back. I don't remember whether this cold remedy worked, but that was part of our early life.

One Christmas season, while writing a note to Santa by candlelight, my hair got singed and I remember Alice being the sister who got a towel or something to put out the fire.

On occasion, Father, who was responsible for the block kitchen, was allowed to go into

Monty Ichinaga, 2003. *Photo: Norman Yamauchi.*

town. He mentioned segregated restroom facilities in the South and that he was instructed to use the ones for the whites. He said that he felt strange about the whole situation.

As I recall, May and Jack did not stay in Jerome since they were able to find jobs (in a candy factory) in Chicago, and Dorothy went to college in Lincoln, Nebraska. Occasionally, May and Jack would send us a big cardboard box of candies and lots of different-colored marshmallows. Needless to say, that was a very big hit with us kids. To be able to get our family out of camp, Father had to find a sponsor who would take responsibility for our family. In February 1944 we moved to our first residence outside camp, in Mitchell, Nebraska.

We first stayed in the basement of a church. My guess is that it was the Sandalls' church. Phoebe remembers that, after we moved in, a cross was burned on the church lawn. Later, we moved into a converted chicken coop on a farm outside of Mitchell, which was owned by a Japanese American, Mr. Yamada. We lived on the farm until November 1944.

Life on the farm was a new experience for us. We helped with the planting, watering, weeding, and harvesting of onions, potatoes, and cabbage. I helped the watering of the crops by watching the water flow down the endless number of rows and identifying the rows in which water was overflowing on the far end. I helped pick up potatoes from the newly overturned potato plants. I remember being put on someone's lap and steering a tractor down one of the rows. The tractor was pulling a trailer, which other family members were loading with freshly cut heads of cabbage. We ate cabbage a lot and, even to this day, I gag at the smell of boiling cabbage. It has just occurred to me that my experience on the farm may be responsible for my not loving onions. I remember that ration coupons were required to purchase many of the family needs for food and transportation.

So ends my memories of life that started in Tulare in 1937, life in the internment camps, farming in Nebraska, and returning home to Tulare in 1946.

Sally K. Idemoto

December 7, 1941—World War II—is when my story started. My story began in Walerga Assembly Center, Tule Lake, Jerome, and Rohwer. This is my story and I am depending on my memory.

San Martin, California

When the word came in 1942 for Japanese families to be sent away to the relocation camps, we were living on a small farm in San Martin, California. I was nine years old and in the fourth grade.

As most families wanted to be together with family members who were living away, our family of seven—my mother, father, grandmother, sister, and two brothers and myself—moved to be with our married sister in Lodi, California.

My oldest brother was drafted into the Army and was already gone. He ultimately became part of the 442nd Regimental Combat Team.

Walerga Assembly Center, California

Our families were sent to Walerga Assembly Center, known also as the Sacramento Assembly Center, which was temporary and open from May 6, 1942, to June 26, 1942. The camp was constructed at a migrant workers' camp fifteen miles northwest of Sacramento. While at Walerga, we got inoculated and lived in barracks with spaces between the boards in the walls. The bathroom was one large outhouse and taking a bath or shower had no privacy. I remember turning ten years of age that summer. From there, we were sent to Tule Lake Relocation Center.

Tule Lake Relocation Center, California

Tule Lake was somewhat better in that the barracks were constructed much better. Because of the camp being built on a dry lake, there was sand everywhere. There were families there from as far as Alaska . . . along with families from California, Washington, Oregon, and possibly Idaho. We had our first snowfall that winter. The song "White Christmas" came out at that time. After a few months, my married sister and her family, along with my father, left for Utah.

So many internees were considered disloyal based on the 1943 loyalty questionnaire. After the "Yes-Yes," "No-No" questionnaire, our family was a "Yes-Yes" family, and was sent to Jerome, Arkansas, and then to Rohwer.

Jerome, Arkansas

We traveled on a train for several days, arriving at Jerome Relocation Center. During our brief stay there, going to the mess hall, I noticed there were young men wearing *geta* sandals. I took it as those individuals might have come from Hawaii. I later learned that many people from Hawaii were sent to Jerome. After a brief stay, the family was transported via truck to Rohwer. Rohwer was about twenty-five miles away.

Rohwer Relocation Center, Arkansas

When we arrived at Rohwer, one of the things I noticed that was different from Tule Lake was that there was a lot of greenery where people had planted flowers and plants between the barracks. There was also a wooden walkway everywhere; I suppose it was to keep from walking on the muddy ground after the rains. I was also surprised that it had snowed that winter. I always thought that the southern states were always warm. Our barrack was on the very edge of the camp next to the forest area. We often took walks among the trees. Unfortunately, as nice as it was, I broke out in a rash after having touched a poison ivy plant.

My sister, who traveled with us to Rohwer, got married to her fiancé who she met while at Tule Lake. After a long time, they joined us in Wisconsin when we left camp.

While I don't remember too much of life in Rohwer, I do remember one family who lived across from our barrack, whose mother was ill and

My sister Clara (left) with my mother in Tule Lake. My sister is wearing the jacket she made in her sewing class in Tule Lake. *From Sakamoto family photos.*

Front row: Grandma, Mom, me, and Dad. Back row: brothers George and Roy. *From Sakamoto family photos.*

was in bed most of the time. I later saw the family back in San Jose after the camp days and was glad to see that she was well.

In the spring of 1944, my father, while working at the cannery in Utah, bought a car and, through the approval of the government authorities, drove to Rohwer to take us out of camp. We moved to a small town in Wisconsin called Elkhorn, where we lived for one year farming and growing vegetables.

Later, I recall that some groups of men came to take photos of our farm, I suppose to show life outside of the camps. As the war was winding down, the authorities were trying to get families to move out of all of the camps. Those photos were a part of a calendar that was put together of the war days.

After one year in Wisconsin, my father, again, drove us to Utah where we stayed for one year. While there, he took a trip back to San Martin, California, talked with several of our friends, and, on returning home, he announced that our friends were all waiting for us to return home. We returned to our small farm in San Martin, back to my friends in the eighth grade and back to our life. We were very fortunate to have somewhere to come home to. Many families did not have that choice.

I dedicate my story to my father, Joseph Uichi Sakamoto, who after getting us back home, two years later, passed away at the young age of fifty-seven from cancer.

Tom Tsutomu Ige

Rohwer Relocation Camp

My name is Tsutomu Ige. Our family—my mother, two brothers, and sister—were sent to Rohwer in October 1942. After three days on the train, I guess I managed OK, being only eleven years old. Went along the Salton Sea, stopped at a station at Ft. Worth, saw the fireflies in the Louisiana forest, and arrived at McGehee station where many Black children were looking straight at us, eating watermelon. I remember seeing photos like that at school. Arrived at Rohwer not far from McGehee. We, from the Santa Anita Assembly Center, were assigned quarters in Block 20. The residents in Block 27 next to ours were from Stockton. Our block was next to a cotton field and I remember going in to pick cotton. Probably because of being close to New Orleans, we had good seafood and sometimes fish I'd never seen or tasted. We had oysters, too, but I think adults and seniors enjoyed them more than we did. Huge watermelons grown by internee farmers in the Delta area were the best.

Most days were spent at the recreation room playing pinochle, ping pong, etc. with newfound friends. We didn't play much outdoors because of the heat and humidity in the summer and cold winter weather. And, since we were the first group sent from Santa Anita, there were no places in our block or anywhere nearby to play outdoor sports. We played in the snow for the first time there, never thinking it would snow in Arkansas. The only snow I saw at Terminal Island was on the snowcapped mountains. The camp was surrounded in the back by forests and swamps, and I never went in for fear of snakes. I saw many rattlesnakes and other snakes, but people who went into the forest told me there were many types and many poisonous snakes. I heard of guys going deep into the forest and who found a canal that looked like a good place to fish. Those who went fishing, mostly for catfish and gar, braved the swamp, snakes, and other swamp dangers. Another craft taken up by the residents was carving figures in new tree stubs growing in the swamp. One popular figure I remember was that of a fish going upstream. I don't think or remember that movies were shown on a regular basis. I saw the one with Frank Sinatra, but can't remember seeing any other. The movie I saw was *Higher and Higher*. I attended church on Sundays. One day a station wagon with soldiers on the top came down the road singing Hawaiian songs, playing their ukuleles. I still remember the song they were singing. Found out they were from Camp Shelby, across the Mississippi River, who came to encourage guys to volunteer.

100th Nisei Unit

One of the saddest days in 1943/44 was when a guy in our block joined the army and was killed in action in Africa about three months later. When I visited the Evergreen Cemetery in Los Angeles and stood in front of the Nisei Memorial, his grave was right in front of me. His name was Tetsuo Yoshizaki, with the 100th Nisei Unit.

I attended school as a sixth grader but can't remember what subjects were taught. The teacher and assistant were both internees. What I remember most is what took place one day in class. Several students got rowdy and when they didn't stop, the teacher shouted "Ben!" "Joe!" and the whole class went into an uproar!

A baby was born in our block in 1943. It was a girl, named Betty, and I didn't see the baby again until 2014. I knew the family well so when I heard one of the sisters passed away, I went to attend her memorial service in Gardena. There I was introduced to another sister and found out she was the baby born in Rohwer. She is now happily married. When I approached her and said, "I remembered you as a baby in Rohwer," she immediately looked surprised and told me, "Don't tell anyone that, I don't want them to know my age!" So, such was my life in Rohwer. Don't remember much more but I'm okay with that.

Fran Inouye Imahara

Fresno Assembly Center

My family of five was living in Fresno, California, located in the Central Valley, when my father received his notice to evacuate to a relocation camp a couple of miles away at the Fresno Assembly Center in 1942. My sister, Nancy, was nine years old; my brother, Allan, was six years old; and I was three years of age. Everyone was in a state of shock, having to leave everything behind. We only had two weeks to gather whatever we could carry into our suitcases. Our family was assigned to the horse stable I-19. Faced with total confusion and fear of the unknown, my father insisted that we take a formal family picture before we had to depart.

Jerome, Arkansas

I was too young to remember much of my experience, but I do recall the long train ride to Jerome, Arkansas. We could not see much because the windows were covered with dark blinds and we were told not to look out. Out of curiosity, I remember peeking and seeing that the train was riding along a river edge close to a big mountain. We were used to hot and dry weather in Fresno and were not used to the cold and wet weather when we arrived in Jerome in October of 1942. We lived in barracks with rooms that housed five families. The barrack walls were covered with tar paper without any insulation. The gaps let in cold air and the floorboards had knotholes that often fell out. Each family had one potbelly stove located in the center of each room and one electrical outlet for lighting.

Tule Lake, California

We were sent to Tule Lake, California, on the Oregon border in September of 1943. [The Tule Lake Relocation Center was located about ten miles south of the town of Tulelake.] Life was as harsh here as at Jerome with winds, rain, and snow with little shelter from the elements in our barracks. Conditions were difficult for all families. My father chopped wood and my mother worked in the mess hall to earn their meager wages along with other families. My family was on the shy and quiet side and again thrown into unfamiliar living conditions. I remember

Frances, 1943.

my mother boiling water to fill a tub to bathe us in our one-room home as she was not comfortable (*hazukashi*) bathing in the open communal facility. We all formed a line daily and ate all our meals in the mess hall. The children would also get their afternoon daily snacks (called *oyatsu*) after they attended Japanese schools.

My father was very artistic, good with his hands, and created projects out of wood. He built cabinets and containers using the tongue and groove techniques since nails were not available. He would make inlaid woodwork with stumps and limbs of trees to form artwork. There were many families with artistic skills. We collected various shells from the dry creeks and the ladies would make beautiful shell pins, and the men made hand-painted wooden bird pins.

Life was not without hardships for our family. My sister, Nancy, got too close to an outdoor bonfire and her clothing accidentally caught on fire. She still has scars on her leg from third-degree burns from the accident. Brother Allan has scars from accidentally cutting his leg from chopping wood. I fell off a stack of boxes into a bucket of boiled water for a bath. We almost lost our father after a serious heart attack from all the stress and chopping firewood. My father wanted us to go to Japan to live after our release and applied for the Japanese citizenship. Relatives advised us there would be nothing for us there. They canceled our request and we returned to Fresno in 1946. We were very fortunate to have a place to return to since a dear family friend, a policeman with the Fresno Police Department, looked after our home.

Now as I look back, I realize the struggles and hardships of camp life for us at Jerome and Tule Lake and the thousands of other internees. However, I am very grateful that my family returned to Fresno and very fortunate to remain a citizen of the United States.

Allan and Nancy, 1942.

Victor Imahara

My name is Victor Imahara. I am seventy-seven years old and I was six months old when the Japanese Air Force carried out an air strike on the US military ships at Pearl Harbor, Hawaii. This action would affect all the Japanese descendants, which included the first, second, and third generation in the United States. I am third-generation Japanese American called Sansei. This is my story.

Florin, California

I went to Sierra Grammar School on Sierra Road in Florin. My mother went to the parent/teacher conference at the school only once. My father did not go because he spoke broken English and was hard to understand. My parents, Yoshio and Kimiko Imahara, were farming grapes and strawberries in Florin, adjacent to Sacramento, California. My father, Yoshio, was born in Japan and my mother was born in California. I was born in Sacramento in 1941. Life in Florin was a dream of my parents and the James M. Imahara family on the sixty-acre farm. My first cousin is Walter Imahara. Walter was four years old in 1941. For most of my life, I did not know Walter very well since his family moved to Louisiana after the war was over. We visited Walter and Sumi during their fiftieth wedding year in 2013. Walter and Sumi live in Baton Rouge and had Imahara's Botanical Garden in St. Francisville. [My wife] Julie and I got to know about the Imahara family in Louisiana and their life after leaving Rohwer, Arkansas. The trip to Louisiana was the beginning of a close relationship between lost cousins. Sumi and Walter visit California each year during the Fourth of July holidays. So, we get together during their annual trip to California to visit family.

After December 7, 1941

Starting in January 1942, those of Japanese descent who lived along the coast were moved into the assembly centers. In preparation, we had to leave our property. We lost all our family possessions. My parents and my brothers and sister were also interned: James, Grace, Tommy, Fred, and Norman. My parents and Walter's parents had a total of sixty acres; farm and equipment were lost and were never to be recovered. I have no memory of those dark days. I don't know what I would have done if I were a grownup. My mother told me that our family was the last to leave Sacramento. My father was a big man and could be very tough protecting the other timid Japanese from the hateful Caucasians. He was over 6'2" with huge hands so he towered over other Japanese men.

Fresno Assembly Center: May–October 1942

My parents said very little of relocation camps. We were put in horse stalls at the Fresno Assembly Center. Some folks were in barracks but not the Imahara families. I was told the weather was very hot and the smell of the horse stables was very bad. I was too young to remember the problems of living in a camp, the food, or the stories of the latrine. I had contracted whooping cough as we were about to leave for Jerome. My mother told me that no doctor would come to see me because of all the resentment towards the Japanese, except a Dr. Smith who was brave enough to come and treat me. My mother did not report my illness to the military because she was afraid that we would be separated. We were put into a special car on the train reserved for sick people.

Journey to Jerome, Arkansas: November 1942–May 1943

I was told the trip by train to Arkansas was for four days and five nights. There were two camps in Arkansas, Rohwer and Jerome, about twenty-five miles apart. The train was very old and very crowded. The black shades had to be drawn except in the desert area. Many of the folks on the train had never been in so many states: California, Arizona, New Mexico, and Texas, all to Jerome internment camp. In Jerome, there were guard towers, fences, and rows and rows of tar-paper buildings. As a child, it was hard to remember the barracks' rooms. The barracks were dusty, and the floor-

Top row: James, Yoshio, and Tommy. *Bottom row:* Fred, Grace, Victor, Kimiko, and Norman.

boards had big gaps between each board where wind and sand would come through. Very shoddy construction. My mother said it was bitter cold in the winter and hot, hot in the summer. But this was the reality of life and we had to *gaman*.

My father was a cook in camp because he had experience as a cook in the Japanese Army. I understand he was paid $12 a month. Nurses and doctors were the highest paid, $19 a month. He also drove and repaired tanks in the Japanese Army, which helped him later with using tractors in farming.

My brother Norman, age eight, told me he and his friends tried to sneak out of camp under the barbed wires to play, and the guards on the tower opened fire with their machine guns toward them. He was never so scared in his life and never tried to sneak out again.

My sister Grace was fifteen years old, and she went to the dances each week that were held in the mess hall. She enjoyed it very much. Out of all this misery, she found a few hours of fun.

Gila River, Arizona

After spending several months in Jerome, we were relocated again to Gila River, Arizona, because German prisoners of war were to be detained in Jerome, instead of the Japanese. Our families were separated at that time. Walter and his family were sent to Rohwer, Arkansas, nearby.

World War II Is Over: August 1945

After the closing of all ten camps in the US, every person had to leave the camps, but many had no place to go home to. As I spoke to many heads of family, this was a very frightening decision on where to go. All persons were given $25 and a ticket to their destination. My father and mother with all their siblings decided to go to Cupertino, California. My older brother James joined the US Army. I remember James telling me that he was sent to Hiroshima as an interpreter and saw the city in ruins. James mentioned the horrible sight. He was soon discharged and returned home. The siblings were so young, we followed the parents and were hoping they made the right decision.

Walter, then age eight, told me that his family was very young and large. With eight children they decided to go to New Orleans. "My father was very bitter," said Walter, "and with no future or money. He had no place to return to in Florin, California. The farm was lost as his future and livelihood were gone." Walter said his parents wanted education for their children, and eight out of nine children went to college later. All four boys joined the military and returned.

Cupertino, California

I remember that I was in the third grade to the ninth grade [before we moved again]. We lived on Prospect Road in Cupertino. My parents sharecropped with twenty other families at Kaiser Ranch, growing strawberries. There were twenty houses in a row, each house identical to the others. We lived in the sixteenth house. My brother, James, sharecropped since no one owned land. While in Cupertino, I had two best friends, Katchure, a Japanese neighbor from the Kaiser camp, and a Caucasian I met during my seventh to ninth grade. My friendship ended when my parents and sibling moved to Sunnyvale. I attended a new high school from the tenth to twelfth grades.

Sunnyvale, California: The Beginning of a Future

My father and James farmed ten acres of strawberries and tomatoes. They pulled large roots from the earth, backbreaking work, before they could plant strawberries and tomatoes. I helped during my college years, which took six years to get my bachelor of science degree. During my farm days, I convinced my parents to open a fruit stand in front of the house. This became a hit with the residents. The stand grew larger each year and more lucrative each year. Soon the profits from the stand were larger than the profits from taking the strawberries and tomatoes to the cannery.

I remember upon graduating from college, I found employment in the high-tech industry. After leaving the farm, I did not see a future in farming. I remember giving my father $20 from my first paycheck and he cried after receiving it. My father said, "My baby has a good job." My salary was $380 per month and was great at that time.

The land which was rented was sold, so we had to move. James, my oldest brother, and his youngest son, Wayne, decided to continue the fruit stand and buy all the fruits and vegetables locally. This was the story of success of Imahara's Produce Store. The store sponsored and donated to many, many events, providing fruits and vegetables to promote the Japanese culture and increase visibility of various Japanese organizations.

Walter Imahara

I, Walter Manabu Imahara, was born on February 14, 1937, to James and Haruka Imahara in Sacramento, California. My new, changed life started on December 7, 1941, and lasted until the end of the war in August of 1945. I was four years old when the war started, so that part of my story began seventy-eight years ago. In early 1942, my parents and their seven children were taken from our sixty-acre grape, strawberry, and chicken farm and sent to the Fresno Assembly Center. The orders for the resettlement came as a consequence of President Roosevelt's Executive Order 9066. Our family was given the number 8663, and I remember that the numbers were placed on all the duffel bags by my sister May. We still have one duffel bag with our name and number printed on it. We were taken by train to Fresno, behind barbed wire, and lived in a horse stable for many months, from May until October. I do remember the horse stable: the smell and the sight of the mattresses filled with hay. When we went to sleep, we all said that "we are hitting the hay." For five-year-olds like me, life was not so bad as we had our parents with us. But do you know what the stables are? They are places for horses and cows to live.

Most of the 5,300 internees were sent to Jerome, Arkansas. I remember hearing my parents speak about where Arkansas was located, and I recall the train ride of five nights and four days. The train was not the best, and the seats were made of wood. The shade was down during the day, but we would take a peek every now and then, and when we did we saw a lot of desert. I remember that when the train finally stopped at Jerome, there was no depot. We all saw barbed wire, sentry towers, and rows and rows of barracks covered in tar paper. Because of our large family, we were given two rooms, twenty feet by twenty feet, with one door and one window. A potbelly stove sat in the middle of the room, and there was one electric cord with a light bulb.

My parents made all of the furniture from leftover lumber from the

Above: Memorial plaque at Fresno Assembly Center.

Left: My name is inscribed on a plaque at the Fresno Assembly Center Memorial.

construction that was still going on around us. We slept on Army cots with heavy wool blankets. Soon the blankets came to be used as room dividers for privacy. I do remember that it was drafty, hot in the summer and cold in the winter. We were told to bring home any tin cans; my father would flatten the cans and use them to cover the holes in the floor.

After we had spent about eighteen months at Camp Jerome, we were transferred to Camp Rohwer, another internment camp that had been constructed at a site about twenty-five miles away. Soon after, Camp Jerome was converted to housing for German POWs. Camp Rohwer was built in the same style as Camp Jerome, near a railroad track, with barbed wire, sentry towers, and the same barracks construction as in Camp Jerome. Because of the length of time we spent in the camps—about three years—I saw families build gardens, as the internees constructed large vegetable gardens to supplement the bad food that was available in the mess hall. I do remember that my father was a block manager and was paid the highest wage, the same as the doctors and other professionals, a wage of $19 a month. My father told me that the internees complained about the food. Soon the potatoes were replaced with rice. I remember that homemade ice cream was made in the mess hall. We all waited for ice cream but many times, salt would get in the ice cream and we thought that was the worst thing that could happen. When the ice cream was good, the elders would give us their ice cream.

As a youngster, the worst experience that I still remember is going to

Guard
tower at
Jerome
Relocation
Center.
*War
Relocation
Authority
photo.*

the latrine. There was a long line of holes with no division, and in a trough under the wooden seats there flowed running water. That was scary, but the worst thing was that the latrine was a long distance from the barracks, and to make the trip in the middle of the night was frightening to me. Many times, I just let nature take its course. My mother and sisters said the worst thing for them was to have to use the latrine and take a shower with no privacy.

I remember that I was in the first grade in Rohwer. My mother took me by the hand and we walked a long way to the school. I told Mom I was not ready for school. During recess, I went back to the barracks, beating my mother home. Next day, again holding me by the hand, she took me to school. This was the beginning of my education. I do remember that we said the Pledge of Allegiance every morning. Many years later, the words "under God" were added.

Some years ago, I was at a funeral in Salt Lake City, and there I met a lady named Joanne Okada. Joanne said that we were in the first grade together. With a lifetime having passed since I remember leaving camp, there was no way I was able to remember her. I met her husband and he said that with her memory, she was able to recall things like that. We both had a photo that had been taken of the first grade in Rohwer, and there we were, both of us, in the photo. We are still good friends after seventy-nine years.

Walter, John, Jun, and Irene in Camp Rohwer.

I recall that after a few months, the guard towers were no longer being manned, and the barbed-wire fence had been left in disrepair. My mother said soldiers were marching with broomsticks. I took my sisters to a grocery store to buy ice cream. I started climbing a guard tower, and fell and broke my arm. I heard my parents and others speak about going to Seabrook Farms in New Jersey. Folks were leaving camp, and my father went for a short time to work in Chicago. I saw a lot of young college-age folks leaving the camp to attend college. The barbed wire was coming down. I was told that during the period in camp, no one escaped. Was it because we looked like the enemy?

The yellow telegram. As a child, I did not know about the yellow telegram, or that the purpose of the Gold Star placed on a family's door was to mark the death in combat of the family's child serving in the war. I still can remember the cry of a mother receiving a yellow telegram. The cry is in my mind forever, and as I write this portion of the story and remember that time, I am filled with emotion.

The war ended in August 1945, and I remember that my parents were in discussion with each other about where to go. The government was going to give each person a train ticket and $25 to a destination of their choice. By this time there were eight children, with May being the oldest at seventeen. My father did not want to go back to California. At the age of thirty-six, he had lost his home and his dignity, and he was bitter

Walter, first row, fourth from right (leaning); Joanne Okada, left of Walter.

against the government. My father mentioned that if he went back, there would be no one to meet him at the train station, no place to live, no relatives, and no future. My father told us about the hatred of Japanese Americans that was still widespread in California. He heard that racist groups in California wanted to take away our citizenship, and send us to Japan at the end of war.

My mother, Haruka Imahara, at age thirty-five, in Camp Rohwer, October 8, 1944.

My parents told us we were going to New Orleans, Louisiana, to start a new life. The phrase *shikata ga nai* was used often; it meant, "it cannot be helped," "it is what it is." I understood later that these words meant the same thing for most of the internees: the internees left camp and they moved forward. First and foremost, my parents were going to educate their children. My father told us many times that education must be first, that education would get you a good job. My father also said, you must live by the rules. Another word, *gaman*, was used often; it simply translates as "perseverance," which means enduring what seems so unbearable with dignity, patience, and quiet strength. At our young age, we did not understand *gaman*.

Life in Louisiana

My father spoke to us often about the decision they had made, wondering whether they had made the right choice by coming to Louisiana; he said to us many times that he "crawled and cried." Life for any Japanese American in America, whether a citizen or not, was very difficult. My father held two or three jobs at a time just to put a roof over our heads and food on the table.

May was the oldest child, so she had to get a job to support the family. May had put "Japanese American" on her job applications, and she had always been denied. Because the South was largely a "Black or White" culture, she began putting "White" on the applications and the jobs began to come. It was a struggle for all the family members. Racial tension was still high, and Louisiana was in a battle between races. We all had racial problems at grade school. I was always small for my age and in the third and fourth grade, I was always being called names and beaten on. There was one boy who was bigger than me, who always called me names and beat on me. When I was on the swing, he would always chase me off. One day, I was prepared, and, in my mind, I had only one chance. I hit him with my fist, and he went down with fear on his face. I stood there prepared to defend myself. The word got around that you may tease me, but I will fight back to win. The word was spread, and I was no longer teased. This action helped my brothers also. I had only one friend in school, Robert Vanderdoes, nicknamed "Cabbage Head," and he spread the word that I would retaliate if attacked. This action helped me to defend myself for a lifetime.

The Rest of the Story

My parents' dream came true and eight out of nine children went to college. Four boys joined the military, and all returned. We started Imahara's Nursery and Landscape Company, and it is still in operation after fifty years.

Above left: I enlisted in the US Army in 1960 and rose to the rank of first lieutenant.

Above right: Sister Lily (left), with me and Sumi.

Right: On a recent visit to the Rohwer camp site.

Addendum

My Japanese American parents' lives were filled with customs, traditions, and values, lives that had been structured by the samurai code passed on by my grandparents, Minezo and Mika Imahara. Both my grandparents had been born in Japan and came to the US; they were first-generation Japanese immigrants and were "aliens ineligible for citizenship." My grandparents were permanent residents of the US, but they never lived long enough to be naturalized when it became allowed by law. My parents believed in the Declaration of Independence, the US Constitution, and the Bill of Rights. Of course, having been born in California, they were very Americanized. We, their children, were Americans as well.

Clover Johnson

The Desert Battalion

Our former neighbor and dear friend, Buck Shaffer, was all about music. He served for many years as the band director for Porterville High School. During WWII he was sent to Muroc Army Air Base (now Edwards Air Force Base) in the Mojave Desert. Buck had led the jazz band at Muroc and played lead alto sax with the group there. He and his band also performed at the nearby bases and service clubs.

Buck was never one to pass up the opportunity to share a fond memory. He told me that Edgar G. Robinson's wife would bring busloads of gals into the desert to dance with the soldiers at the service club where he played regularly. She would enlist girls who were office workers and telephone operators from the Los Angeles area to visit not only Muroc, but other military installations as well. Buck was thankful for these "Desert Battalion" girls, as he said Mrs. Robinson would call them. He found it encouraging to see the men having such a good time because of those volunteers. Supporting the troops was what Buck was all about, whether it was providing the music for dances, marching around the base, or playing on the flight line.

Jerome Relocation Camp

I told Buck that my Aunt Gertrude had been part of a "Desert Battalion" of sorts, too. The Jerome relocation camp (Jerome, Arkansas), where she and the rest of the Nagata family had been sent, had a Hospitality Center for servicemen. Aunt Gertrude, or "Gertie" as she was called, and her friends worked there to welcome the soldiers, serving coffee and refreshments and holding dances. I also told Buck that my father wasn't too crazy about the idea of his little sister dancing with "strange soldier boys."

"Gertie" Nagata (far left) and her friends standing in front of a sign that says, "Welcome soldiers."

Buck laughed when I told him my aunt married one of those soldiers, Fred Watanabe.

People sometimes concluded that Buck Shaffer wasn't good at remembering names; he had the habit of calling all his female students "little gal" instead of using their names. But even if he didn't recall names, Buck deeply appreciated people who helped others. And he never forgot the efforts of ordinary folks who went out of their way to make a soldier feel important—like the "little gals" who volunteered to serve in Mrs. Robinson's "Desert Battalion."

Even in a relocation center, my Aunt Gertrude and her friends were proud to support the soldiers, too.

The Face of the Enemy

My uncle, Harry Nagata, was already in the service when Pearl Harbor was bombed. He was drafted into the US Army in February of 1941 and

The YWCA and USO Hospitality Center at the Jerome Relocation Center. Note the smiling faces of the servicemen. Gertrude Nagata is on the far left.

went to Fort Ord. After the war began, he was sent to Fort Leavenworth, Kansas, where he worked in the motor pool. About a year and a half later he was ordered to language school at Camp Savage–Fort Snelling, Minnesota. He also served at Fort Meade and Fort McClellan before being discharged at Fort McArthur in February of 1946.

I have written many stories about World War II as they were told to me by those who lived through that time. Oddly, this story was never told to me directly. Harry Nagata was a very talkative, friendly guy—and he told me many stories—but he really never discussed his time in the service with me. A lot of what I know about it comes from things my dad and sister have shared with me.

My father, Milton Nagata, felt like his younger brother was often given the worst duties—the dirtiest jobs—while serving in the army. Digging ditches. Cleaning grease pits. Latrines. Stuff no one else wanted to get stuck doing. I've heard that in one unit he drove mule teams—supposedly to save rubber tires and gasoline for the war effort.

Growing up in Lindsay, California, Harry Nagata was an ordinary farm boy. He went to Sunday school. Rode his bike around. Fixed up old cars and motorcycles. Later he worked in farm labor camps around the state. He was good-natured and hardworking. Harry liked American

Harry Nagata on leave, visiting his family and friends at the Jerome Relocation Center. Harry is in uniform on the right. His brother, Milton, is in the center.

music and Mexican food. One time he jokingly told me that he wished he'd been born into a Hispanic family because he liked tamales and enchiladas so much.

I don't know where the following incident took place, but while Harry was in the service in the Midwest or on [the] East Coast, he encountered fellow soldiers who had never seen anyone of Japanese ancestry before. Someone in command decided it would be hard for the men to fight an enemy they'd never seen. Harry Nagata was ordered to dress up in the uniform of a Japanese soldier and parade in front of the troops so they could see and hate "the face of the enemy." Needless to say, that was a horrible thing to do to a loyal American soldier and it breaks my heart every time I think about it.

Uncle was kind and helpful and cheerful and positive as I remember him, but I wonder if that experience scarred him deep inside. One time after he'd had a bad stroke and was in a wheelchair, we were talking about his health. He said he felt like his doctor usually rushed him out of the office and didn't spend any time listening to his concerns. "Oh, well, maybe it's because I'm Japanese," he said in conclusion.

Harry Nagata passed away in January 2004—less than a year after he lost his wife, Kay, and two weeks short of his ninety-fourth birthday. He was buried with military honors. It was a cold and foggy day, but a local group of veterans showed up to honor one of their own. Harry's coffin was draped with an American flag that was carefully folded and handed to his son, Bill. A lone bugler played and there was a three-gun salute. As the rifle shots echoed across the cemetery, I hoped my dad and uncle could hear them in heaven and know that, even when some people get it wrong, so many others get it right.

An American soldier and his son: Harry Nagata holding his boy, "Billy."

I'll Always Remember

Hard to believe now, but I was born in Tulare, California, in 1958—only thirteen years after World War II ended. I grew up hearing stories about life during the war. I was blessed to have two parents who were both avid storytellers. They had the ability to help me see what they saw and feel what they felt without ever leaving my home. Because Mom (Suzushiro Sekiguchi) was in Japan and Dad (Milton Nagata) was in the United States at that time, I was able to get two different perspectives—see two different worlds.

My mother's parents left her in Tokyo to study before the war broke out. Since she could not return to the US, she didn't go to the Jerome Relocation Center with her parents and siblings. She attended school there in Japan, became a schoolteacher, and served as a translator when the occupation forces arrived at the end of the war. I have often wondered what would have happened if my grandparents had been warned that war was coming. Had they known, my mom (Suzushiro) would have returned to California with her family. Her parents had gotten a job teaching at the Lindsay Nihon Gakko. After Japan bombed Pearl Harbor, she would have gone to the Fresno Assembly Center and then to Jerome. She would have been a high school student at the time. Because of her proficiency in Japanese and English, she might have gone on to language school and served as a translator or even a language instructor for the US military.

Like the Sekiguchi family, the Nagata family of Tulare also went to Jerome, Arkansas. My dad was thirty-four years old in 1942. In a way, he

Interpreter Suzushiro Sekiguchi (front row, second from left), with coworkers and soldiers from the occupation forces.

had become the head of his household. His Issei parents didn't speak much English and weren't young. Grandpa (Fred Nagata) was in his late sixties when he was interned. Dad's older brother Karl had a family of his own and went to Manzanar. Brother Harry was already in the army. That left Milton to care for the family farm, his parents, and his four younger sisters.

As it turned out, my parents did not meet and marry each other until years after the war even though their two families were acquainted and shared camp experiences. There was a seventeen-year age difference between my father and mother. In camp, Dad was active in camp operations as an electrician and a truck driver for the co-op. With a stubborn father and four single sisters, Dad had his hands full caring for his own family and was not looking for a wife at the time. Had she gone to Jerome, my mother would have been a teenager, attending school and staying busy with the activities that occupied other girls her age. Milton and Suzushiro probably would have met but wouldn't have interacted socially because of the age gap. I don't know if they would have ever gone on to marry.

At the walnut farm where I grew up, I was surrounded by constant reminders of my family history. The redwood trees themselves were souvenirs of trips my dad and his brothers had taken into the mountains. Dad enjoyed sharing his experiences and insights. He could walk by an old truck or a fruit tree or even the old outhouse and have a tale to tell. The walnut orchard itself was a story of how World War II affected the Nagata family. The family was forced to leave for camps before the young trees could be grafted. As a result of being grafted late when the war ended, the trees had dark, black walnut trunks with thick bark instead of smooth, light-colored trunks like all the other English walnut trees in the

Boards from crates that were used while my grandparents were interned were later used to make a lid for a box that stored walnut sacks on the farm.

area. In the shed, Dad stored things in wooden packing crates, marked with War Relocation Center addresses. From time to time he'd talk about what life was like in "Camp." Scattered about the farm were tiny reminders of life in "Camp": hand-carved wooden clothespins with "Nagata" written on each one. Odd and interesting pieces of wood collected in the desert. A beautiful, hand-polished cane. Wooden *geta*, also hand-carved, but missing the straps to be complete. A blanket with the family name and number embroidered on the binding. Old letters and postcards. A high school yearbook sent to camp by friends of my aunts.

Grandma Momoye, my father's mother, lived with us and was part of my earliest memories. I regret never letting her teach me how to crochet doilies and make rag rugs, skills I think she learned in Jerome. I never got to meet my Grandpa Nagata. He had a disabling stroke and passed away in 1947 at the age of seventy-two. Since many of my relatives lived into their eighties or even nineties, I kind of felt like my grandpa died "young." Maybe it's not true, but I think he would have lived a longer, happier life if he had stayed on his farm and not been sent to Arkansas. I told my father once that I wished I'd gotten to know his father. "Eh, you didn't miss much," he said with a grin.

While my parents were still with us, I made an effort to really listen and write down their recollections so they would be remembered. I have also been fortunate to be able to spend time with my mother's brother, Joh Sekiguchi, and have him tell me about life in the Jerome Relocation Center. I hope reading what I've written will allow you to feel like you're sitting around the farmhouse table and hearing stories like they were told to me.

Dear Lois: Miyo Machigashira

My Aunt Lois and her friend, Miyo, both seniors, had to leave Tulare for the Fresno Assembly Center in May of 1942. They were not able to participate in the end-of-school activities and graduate with other (non–Japanese American) classmates at Tulare Union. Among the treasures that were stored at the old farm were two Tulare Union High School yearbooks from 1942. They both belonged to my Aunt Lois and appear identical on the outside. The difference lies in the autographs on the inside.

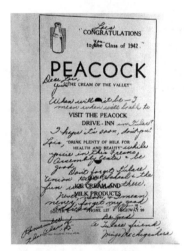

Miyo Machigashira (also from Tulare) used this ad as part of her message. This yearbook was autographed in Fresno after it was sent to my aunt. *Tulare Union High School Argus—1942.*

Photos of Miyo and Lois from the TUHS yearbook 1942. The Nagata and the Machigashira families both returned to Tulare to farm after the war. *Tulare Union High School Argus—1942.*

CLOVER JOHNSON

The Sewer Farmer

Life in the Jerome relocation camp was difficult for everyone. There was very little privacy. Sometimes large families or groups were crowded into one-room "apartments" in barracks buildings that had thin walls and no insulation. Twelve of these buildings made up a block which could house 250 to 300 people. The laundry, shower, and toilet facilities were shared by everyone who lived on that block. Each block had its own dining hall, too. So, if you wanted to take a shower or eat breakfast—or just use the toilet—you had to venture out to the group facility and hope there wasn't a long line. The climate didn't make things easier. Summers were hot and humid. Winters were mild, but there could still be frost on the ground. The frequent rains often turned the camp into a sea of mud. People had to lay down boards to cross the ditches and gullies that formed when the place flooded.

With the frequent rains, surrounding swamps were an ideal home for mosquitoes. They would buzz around in huge, dark swarms, biting people and spreading disease. The food wasn't always the freshest or of the best quality, either. All this could make it easy for people to get sick. Colds, influenza, and other illnesses could spread like crazy. For the very young and the elderly, staying well wasn't easy.

While in the Jerome camp, my father worked as an electrician. He also worked in the co-op, driving a truck. Some of his friends worked in agriculture there. My Aunt Gertrude volunteered to help local servicemen. I think my aunt Lois worked as a nurse's aide. At that time, my

Doris Sato poses on a makeshift wooden bridge across a ditch with rainwater near Block 16.

Hisashi Hayakawa at work at the Jerome Relocation Center water treatment facility.

Uncle Harry was in the US Army. My Uncle Karl went to the Manzanar Relocation Center where he was a pharmacist. I was proud of the things they all did despite their circumstances. And then there was Hisashi Hayakawa, who married my Aunt Florence. Uncle Hisashi worked at the Jerome camp "sewer farm." Not a very glamorous job, to say the least. As a kid, I used to think that was funny and wondered why he didn't find something better to do. Looking back, I finally realize that it wasn't anything to laugh at. In such a hot, swampy, crowded place that teemed with insects, good sanitation—and keeping the drinking water from getting contaminated—must have been critical.

So, thank you, Uncle Hisashi. Sorry I didn't appreciate what you did sooner.

Atsuko Shimasaki Kusuda

My strongest memory of evacuation was that I was a loyal American citizen. That's how I felt. I cried and cried because they treated me like an enemy alien by putting me in an internment center. My heart was broken.

December 7, 1941

My father had passed away in December 1941 just before Pearl Harbor. I was glad that he didn't see the war between America and Japan.

I had just finished Porterville Junior College in California. I had talked to the dean because I was an "A" student, but I had to leave before the semester was over. It was the last month of school, June, before I completed my two years. So, the dean gave me credit for the full two years but dropped all my grades to a "B."

Fresno Assembly Center

We went to the Fresno Assembly Center, then to Jerome, Arkansas. I remember putting straw in mattresses. I made peace with the fact that I was there. Now I think I've said enough. I don't want to be asked any more questions about it.

Jerome and Rohwer Relocation Camps

Later in camp, there was a meeting put on by the American Friends Service Committee for just about five to ten of us girls who were high school graduates. They asked us what we wanted to do. I said I wanted to go to college and that I already had two years of junior college in California before we were evacuated. The American Friends Service Committee got in touch with the YWCA and I was given a scholarship. I applied to the University of Missouri because I thought it would be better than an Arkansas school, and the National YWCA paid my tuition.

I was in the first group of people to be released from Rohwer, which was only individuals. Later, everyone was released.

Atsuko Shimasaki Kusuda.

Grace Imahara Marubashi

Fresno Assembly Center

We were taken to Fresno racetrack, converted into Fresno Assembly Center, since this was a temporary stay, about six months. Life was very difficult, and I remember our family was given mattresses filled with straw. We stayed in a horse stable.

Jerome Relocation Center

After six months we were transferred to the relocation center in Jerome, Arkansas. Mom worked as a waitress for $16 a month. Since [my brother] Katsu was still just a few months old, I took Mom's place in the morning until I went to school. Then she would come and finish the work, leaving Katsu with a neighbor lady. In the evening I took over till closing time in the mess hall. On weekends if there was dancing nearby, I went with my boyfriend Sam. I learned how to jitterbug, which was fun. Dad was a chef at $19 month. I was a junior in high school and graduated in 1944 at Jerome. Since Jerome Relocation Center was closing, the rest of the Imahara family was transferred to another camp about twenty-five miles away called Rohwer Relocation Center.

Gila River Relocation Center, Arizona

After Rohwer, our family was transferred to Gila River, Arizona. I worked as clerk, stenographer, [and] block and manager's helper. Once a week Sam and I went to a movie, which was out on a hillside. We took blankets to sit on not-so-comfortable grass and rocks and enjoyed the movies. Another time on a weekend our office group had an outing and went out on the desert nearby. While we were leaning against the rock, out of nowhere a big tarantula came out and landed on one of the girl's arms. We swatted this monster spider and fortunately she wasn't bitten. I kept busy after work and once a week I had to go to sewing school. I learned to draft patterns so I can make and design my own wardrobe. It was fun drafting my own patterns and making my own outfits. Some came in handy when I made several dresses for Linda, my daughter. I went out to Ogden, Utah, for seasonal work until the war was over.

Grace Imahara Marubashi.

Sacramento, California

We came home to Taishoku [Florin, California] and helped with strawberry picking until my marriage to George Marubashi in 1947. When I married George, he had a tomato field farm. After tomato season was over, we moved to Sacramento and he found a job at Campbell Soup Company where he worked for thirty-two years. He also worked for Mr. Oshima in the morning, who handled strawberries and other fruits. He went to work for Mr. Oshima right after his work until time to work at Campbell Soup. Don't know how he did it with so little sleep. Of course, strawberry season was not too long. Anyways, after we bought our first home, I said I will work until the house was paid up, which was twenty-five years when Linda, Larry, and Lesley were grown up and left home. I was a night widow, so I decided to take some night courses, something like judo lessons for self-defense, for about five to six years. I found another class which was combined with judo and karate. I stuck with judo to help with teaching new students. I received *Sankyū* (third-rank brown belt). While there I also went and took belly dancing and auto mechanic for two semesters, which came in handy. I also had a hand in Tupperware for a few years, Share Gold, and Amway for several years. But one of my good friends deals directly with headquarters in Michigan even now, as she needs these products to keep in good health.

George retired from Campbell Soup after thirty-two years and I also retired from the Department of Motor Vehicles. I wasn't restless for too long when Linda said there were a couple of sisters who wanted to study the Bible with a Japanese person. I told them in the beginning that I didn't want to be a Jehovah's Witness, that I just wanted to know about the Bible. I soon learned a lot of things I was doing wrong. I finally decided to get baptized in 1986 after five or six years of studying. George passed away in April 1991. A group of Jehovah's Witnesses were going on a tour to New York Headquarters, so I signed up to go and see. It was a very educational tour. We saw how they printed the *Watchtower* and *Awake!* magazines and how they raised their own vegetables and dairy for meat and milk products. After the tour in New York, my friend, Kazuko, and I went to Japan and stayed for a week and visited with her sister in Shizuoka. They took us on a tour, and we saw Mount Fuji close by. Kazuko and I went on our tour by bullet train to other cities nearby. We also went to visit Isamu, my cousin, in Hachioji near Tokyo on the bullet train. He treated us to a homemade udon dinner he prepared. His wife, Asako, showed us a tea ceremony briefly. That was the first and last visit to Japan. I had no problem speaking Japanese for shopping. They thought I came back to Japan to visit.

George worked at Campbell Soup Company for thirty-two years and I worked at the Department of Motor Vehicles for twenty-five years. George passed in 1991 after forty-four years of marriage. I was ninety-three in October 2019.

Caroline Matsuyama

Fresno Assembly Center

Before arriving at the Jerome Relocation Center, we had already spent five months incarcerated at the Fresno County Fairgrounds in hastily built barracks to accommodate us "evacuees" (as we were called). This was also known as the Fresno Assembly Center for the duration of our stay there.

It was a great relief to learn we would be well treated, providing we did not try to escape. We were told they were protecting us from the public, but all the guns were facing inward, and none outward. Every night at around ten o'clock, a soldier would come to our room to take roll . . . to make sure no one was missing.

Jerome, Arkansas

When it came time to move from the Assembly Center to our more permanent location, they herded us into old Pullman trains and instructed us to pull down our shades, so no one could see us. I don't recall how many days it took to get to our destination, but it was several l-o-n-g days, something like three or four days. We were not told where we were going, so it was a big surprise we ended up in Arkansas.

As we arrived at the relocation center, we noticed our barracks were still being built, so we were able to converse with some of the workers on the job. The Jerome Relocation Center was built in the swamplands, so the roads that separated the blocks were elevated, with drainage ditches on each side. This kept the people from roaming into another block without a good reason. Our family and close friends were in the same block, so we were able to visit with them often. However, we hardly ever had our family meals together, which was unfortunate. Since the plan was to keep us locked up for the duration of World War II, schools—elementary and high schools—needed to be in the planning. Prior to the evacuation, I had spent a little over one semester at Fresno State College as a music major, so they placed me as the accompanist for the high school choir, under the direction of Ms. Mary Kasai, music teacher from Fresno. She was well liked by the students and the class was fun.

The rest of my employment was spent as a stockroom clerk, handing out supplies requested by the teachers. Marian Imamoto was the other stockroom clerk; in fact she was already in charge, so you can say I was her assistant. This stockroom was also an (unplanned) meeting place for the Nikkei teachers to relax between classes to discuss the world's problems or whatever was on their minds. It resembled a teacher's lounge . . . without chairs or sofas . . . only boxes to sit on. It was an enjoyable job, where we became well acquainted with the teachers.

After the residents became more settled, churches were being organized. . . . There was a merger of several Christian Protestant denominations to form one church, which our family and friends attended. We would have services on Sunday mornings where we could meet and make new friends, which I thought was very nice. There were many good leaders and singers who showed up in this group.

During our first Christmas in Jerome, the leaders decided to sponsor a Christmas play. I don't remember the title of the play, but it was about a family whose children did not have the true Christmas spirit. Well, I was one of the spoiled brats in that play, sorry to say, but it was fun!

Late in the spring and summer months we noticed there were Nisei soldiers coming to Jerome to visit friends and family. I believe they were stationed at nearby Camp Shelby. It didn't take long before Ms. Mary Nakahara organized a USO group of young women to greet and entertain the visiting soldiers. With the enthusiastic energy she placed in this club, I'm sure it was a most successful venture!

My residency at the Jerome Relocation Center ended much sooner than expected. It was just ten months since our family first arrived at Jerome. I never thought at that time I would ever feel sadness to leave Jerome, but I remember having shed some tears. In fact, it was my first time leaving "home." My parents and an older sister remained in camp; they would join us in Minneapolis at a later date.

After having met so many wonderful friends and being involved in interesting activities, camp life was not so bad. In fact, it was an interesting place to live, for the young folks. It was the Issei (first-generation

Japanese) who suffered the most from the "Evacuation." Many who were forced to leave their homes on short notice had little time to sell their valuables at ridiculously low prices, or some were just given away.

When the camps closed in 1945, many of the evacuees had no place to go . . . some families camped out at their former churches, until they could find a better place to live . . . They needed to find employment or start a business of their own. It was a difficult time for many and especially for the elderly. Sadly, many of the older Issei did not live long enough to receive their letter of apology and long-overdue "Reparations," awarded by the US government to only the living survivors. Both of my parents (sadly) did not live long enough to receive these awards.

Caroline Matsuyama in Minneapolis, 1944.

Lily Imahara Metz

Every story has a beginning and end. In order to connect to my 3½ years spent in the US relocation camps, a long journey is needed to get from there to here. I remember when my parents, James and Haruka Imahara, with their seven children (under sixteen years of age), were driven to the Florin Train Station. It was good-bye to our home life in Sacramento, California. I was seven years old.

We arrived at the Fresno Assembly Center and stayed in horse stalls on the Fairgrounds for over four months in 1942. We boarded a huge black steam-driven train and traveled for four days and five nights. During this time, we were told not to raise the darkened blinds on the window. I broke the rules and peeked out. I saw many wigwams and Indians. Later in grade school in camp, I drew what I saw, and the teacher was shocked. She said that I saw an Indian reservation and the wigwams were their homes.

The train stopped in Jerome, Arkansas. Strangely, there was no train station. I saw rows and rows of unfinished black tar-paper shacks. We were given a twenty-by-twenty-foot room with cots, hay mattresses, and a woodstove. There was one light bulb in the center of the room. The family stayed in Jerome more than a year, until the government decided to relocate German prisoners of war to the camp. I cannot recall anything of this period.

What I do remember is one day when I climbed in the back of a cattle truck along with my family, and we were taken to another camp about twenty miles away near the town of McGehee, Arkansas. This would be our home for eighteen months and the remainder of the war. This place provided life-changing experiences and left me with lasting mental and emotional hurts and hangups. Being a Japanese American was very hard on my parents and family members, including myself.

Barracks. *Sketch by Lily Imahara Metz.*

I did find opportunity for my personal growth at the library, and I read to my heart's content. Books opened a whole new world for me. We walked everywhere. A vivid image is the dirt or soil where I walked in my bare feet. The ground was so dry that the earth cracked open and left spaces that hurt my feet. I learned there can be suffering even in pleasure.

The entertainments included outdoor movies, and my favorite movie stars were Van Johnson, Roy Rogers, Gene Autry, and Esther Williams. There was a stage in a large building where musicals and dramas were performed by residents. The stage was hand-painted with panoramic scenes of camp life at the top of the wall and on all sides except the stage. I watched sumo wrestling and baseball games. I participated in Obon dancing at Japanese festivals, and other entertainment, which were all fascinating and exciting to a young country girl.

I remember walking around the blocks and watching men doing woodwork, carving, polishing, and creating beautiful pieces of artwork. I remember lampstands made from cypress knees. The work was creative and original. Many years later in life, I saw a lamp made of a cypress knee with a shade at a craft show and I bought it. I enjoyed watching the ladies and young girls doing needlework, sewing, knitting, and crocheting. I watched my older sister, Flora, design a beautiful piece of needlework, which hangs today in her living room in California.

We had Christmas in camp, and we received apples, oranges, and candy canes along with milk and cookies. I remember standing on the mess hall table and singing Christmas songs such as "Jingle Bells," "Frosty the Snowman," and others. The mess hall, I recall, was very strange. I was used to eating in the kitchen back home with Mom cooking and serving regular food, and parents and children eating together. Now we ate in a mess hall with dozens of strangers, and usually without family members.

Lastly, I remember the sentry towers with guards carrying rifles. We must have lived close to the barbed-wire fence, and it seemed to stretch around the entire camp. At one time, I crawled under the fence with my brother Walter and sister Jane to go to a nearby store on the outside. Thoughts of camp life remind me of who we were and why we were there. Many questions with no answers.

Guard tower. *Sketch by Lily Imahara Metz.*

The ending of my camp life was as abrupt as the beginning. I remember that I was four years older when my world became quite a bit more complicated and disarrayed. My parents decided to relocate to Louisiana after the war ended and we were set free. The reason for this life-changing decision was based on the future of their eight children, the need to get higher education.

Our first real house since before the war was in a strange city called New Orleans, and it became our home for a few years. During this time, we faced prejudices and discrimination and unfairness in our surroundings. As my father said, "I cried and crawled every day to make a living." There was only a handful of Japanese Americans in the South.

Then our family moved to the country and did share crop farming. We were able to stay in touch with special friends, like the Okubo and Sagawa families, as well as Mrs. Nasu, a close friend whose family raised tomatoes, made a fortune, and returned to California. These families were our support group, and we helped each other in the true Buddhist way and Christian living.

Pop eventually was hired as head gardener for a plantation home in St. Francisville, located in central Louisiana. Here Pop was able to ground himself and begin to heal from the loss made by war. Shortly thereafter, Pop and Mom moved the family to the capital and university city of

Lily Imahara Metz in April 2019 at the memorial to Japanese American soldiers at the former site of the Rohwer Relocation Center.

Baton Rouge for work opportunities and to rebuild the family business. God blessed our family, and all the Imahara children graduated from college. All four sons served in the US armed forces and returned home. I remained in St. Francisville, and my husband and I raised a bountiful family of seven children. As I have been told, it is not what happens to us that matters, but how we come out of it.

Milton Nagata

At Home on the Range

With the Jerome Relocation Center closing in June of 1944, we had to decide where to go next. Some of the people joined the service or found jobs outside the camps. That was permitted if you avoided working in certain areas—like on the West Coast. Most of us chose between the remaining nine camps. My sister Florence and her husband Hisashi decided to go to Gila River, Arizona. That made our mother want to go there, too, so she went to the camp office and signed up for Gila. Our father, however, decided to go to Granada, Colorado, since he had relatives farming in that state. He went to the camp office and found their names were already on the Gila list. Dad assumed a mistake had been made and changed it to Granada. Later, Mom went by the camp office and found their names on the Granada list. Also thinking a mistake had been made, she switched back to Arizona. This went back and forth before someone got wise to what was going on. Mom didn't want to leave Florence, but Dad eventually won.

We left the muggy, snake-infested swamps behind and moved west to Granada, Colorado. Granada was actually the small town located near the relocation center. The postal designation of the area was Amache, so the camp was also called Amache Center. (This area was named after the Cheyenne Indian woman who had married the rancher John Prowers. Later, the county was named after him and became Prowers County.)

Granada was located about fifteen miles west of the Kansas border on a windswept prairie. The land sloped northward towards the Arkansas

As told to Clover Johnson by Milton Nagata (1908–1995).

River where cottonwoods could be found along the banks. It was fairly dry all around the camp, though. Wild grass, sagebrush, and prickly pear cactus grew. At an elevation of 3,600 feet, temperatures could drop quite a bit during the night. Those of us who had come from Central California were somewhat familiar with range land and horse and cattle ranches, but the area was still more rugged than what we were used to.

There was one guy who was completely at home there on the range. I don't know where he'd learned, but boy, could he ride! Instead of bouncing up and down on horseback like many people I've watched, he could really move with the animal. He'd become good friends with the local Indians, and they'd come to the camp with a spare horse to take him out riding on the prairie. Well, as I recall they got really late getting back once. He and his buddies rode up to the camp gate sun-browned, dusty, and sweaty. The guards took one look at them and told them all to get lost. They assumed they were Indians looking for a handout or just looking to cause trouble. Well, he had a heck of a time convincing the MPs that he lived there and that his friends were just trying to return him before he got in trouble. I think he even had to send for his block captain before they let him back in.

Unfortunately, he was not the only guy who had problems with the camp guards. Our own father ran into trouble for violating curfew. One night the guards picked him up for getting too close to the fence and hauled him into the police station. Thank goodness they did not shoot first and ask questions later. No, Dad was not trying to escape. He was just trying to pee. You see, none of the individual living quarters had their own bathrooms, so you had to use the community facilities. During the night when you were supposed to stay inside, you had to use a bucket or chamber pot if you had to "go." Whole families shared a living space and there was not much privacy. Well, our father was stubborn as a mule and insisted on going outside to relieve himself when it was against the camp rules. He was very lucky to know people with some influence who were willing to speak up to the authorities on his behalf.

With the exception of Tule Lake, the remaining eight camps officially closed in October or November of 1945. Fortunately, we had a home to return to, thanks to Adolph Feilbach, our attorney. He made certain that we did not lose title to our property while we were gone. I returned to California ahead of the rest of my family to get the house and farm ready for them.

Our neighbor Mrs. Kazarian took care of me until they came home. I appreciated the meals, so I did not complain, but boy, was her Armenian coffee strong! And her mustard-pickled eggplant packed quite a kick. Talk about bitter—I could never eat ripe olives right off the tree like the Kazarians could.

I thought I'd left the bayous behind in Arkansas, but I was wrong. I returned to Tulare to find a swamp that was—of all places—under our house. Before the war my father had started digging below his bedroom. We had a small, concrete-lined cellar with shelves where we stored canned goods, but after seeing a friend's large basement, Dad decided he wanted something room-sized, too. Every evening he'd go down there and dig and come out covered with dirt from head to toe. We had to leave the farm before he could complete the project. While we were gone, the gophers had a field day. They tunneled between the house and a nearby ditch. When the ditch was filled with irrigation water, guess where the water flowed? Yep. The soft soil washed out, leaving quite a pit. I had to put in wooden braces that were quite tall to keep the house supported.

Things could have been in a whole lot worse shape without our neighbors the Kazarians keeping an eye on our place. Still, they let their cattle graze in the vineyard and the vines got in pretty sad shape. We were planning to eventually take the vineyard out anyway, but not until the walnuts started producing. The black walnut trees that we'd interplanted were overgrown because we weren't there to graft them on schedule. I went ahead and grafted them late anyway and was glad that the English walnuts took. At least those cows provided good fertilizer, because our vegetables grew exceptionally large the next season.

Farming in Jerome? No Thank You!

During World War II, the government built relocation camps for the Japanese in some of the most desolate parts of the country. Japanese Americans were first sent to assembly centers—at places like racetracks and fairgrounds—while the more permanent facilities were being hurriedly thrown together. Our family was living in Tulare, California, in 1942. When we were sent to the Fresno Assembly Center we had to leave a vineyard full of grapes unharvested. They turned the Tulare Fairgrounds into an assembly center, too, and moved people up from Southern California to stay there. Those poor folks from Los Angeles weren't used to the 100-plus-degree temperatures like we were.

Even then, the summer weather here in the Valley could seem mild

Milton Nagata's camp pin-back buttons. The temporary assembly centers, like the one at the Fresno Fairgrounds, were under the control of the Army's Wartime Civil Control Administration. Relocation centers, like the one in Jerome, were under the War Relocation Authority.

compared to the extreme heat found in places like Poston, Arizona. On top of the heat, the Japanese sent to the camp there also suffered from choking dust storms. And although we got dense fog and frost in Tulare, it rarely snowed. Camps like Heart Mountain could get buried in snow. Jerome, Arkansas, where many of the Japanese from Tulare County went, didn't have those particular problems; it had others—like mosquito-filled swamps and poisonous snakes.

It was a long train ride, halfway across the country to Arkansas. While we were traveling through that state, I began to wonder if we'd even arrive at the relocation center at all. The Mississippi River seemed at flood stage. The muddy water was so wide and high in spots it even seemed to be lapping at the train tracks. I was afraid the rickety wooden supports would collapse beneath us and we'd all be drowned.

Somehow the train finally did arrive at the Jerome camp. The barracks there were an improvement over the barns and horse stalls that people had been staying in at the assembly centers. Still, when it started to rain, some of the roofs leaked and the whole area became a sea of mud. The camp had been hastily built in about three months and many parts of it were not yet completed. Many people formed work crews to make the place livable. When the Jerome center reached maximum, over eight thousand people were detained there.

Since I'd been a farmer, one of my friends came to me and told me some of the guys were starting an agricultural project. He was going to sign up and invited me to join in. Well, one look around told me that

MILTON NAGATA

farming there was going to be no piece of cake. Before they could even think of planting anything, land had to be cleared and swamps had to be drained—all while fighting the rain and mud or heat and humidity, not to mention swarms of hungry mosquitoes. To make matters worse, there were poisonous snakes everywhere. They could even fall out of the trees onto you. Farming in Jerome? No thank you.

Instead, I drove a truck for the camp co-op, going into town to get supplies. The other thing I decided to do was become an electrician. I'd never worked in a radio or appliance shop before, but no one had to know that. They needed people to fix radios and small electrical appliances like toasters and irons and fans, so that's what I did. Sometimes the fancier a radio was advertised to be, the easier it was to fix. A lot of the tubes and gizmos inside were just there for looks—they didn't do anything, so when the basic parts gave out, they could be used as spares.

Besides small repairs, there was plenty of electrical work for us to complete along with camp upkeep. I learned to climb power poles to make connections. There were no mechanical lifts, but it wasn't too hard if you had the right gear.

The real headache to knowing wiring was getting stuck helping to set up—and take down—the lighting and PA systems for some of the special entertainment. The musical programs weren't too bad; many of the singers were very talented—like the Nomura sisters from Lindsay. I remember they had lovely voices and were quite popular with the young men. Unfortunately, the sumo matches often became just plain silly. A lot of women liked to attend. They didn't actually appreciate the sport; they just went to giggle at the wrestlers—especially when "things" slipped out of place. The homemade *fundoshi* or loincloths exposed enough to begin with. To make matters worse, they weren't made of the sturdiest material. Sure, you could get disqualified for doing things to your opponent's loin-cloth, but heck, it didn't matter if you had no shot at winning anyway. Besides, such mishaps were sure to please the crowd.

Working in the radio shop kept me out of the worst of the weather, but it could still be hot and muggy inside. I heard that hospital workers liked to eat their lunches down in the morgue because in the summer that was the coolest spot in the entire camp. Jerome was subject to terrible thunderstorms. I learned just how dangerous they could be—even if you were indoors. The entire camp was divided into smaller sections called blocks. The blocks had their own mess halls and shower and toilet

Above: Clearing land and chopping wood at the Jerome Relocation Center.

Right: Milton Nagata (on the right) and fellow electrician posing in front of the Jerome Relocation Center Radio and Electric shop.

facilities. One time, lightning struck a chimney or metal vent pipe on one of the buildings. The bolt came down and, not having any place to go, "danced" several feet across the floor before finding its way down a drain. It actually burned the concrete along its path, leaving a black scar. Fortunately, no one was in its way or they would have been killed. I think they put up lightning rods after that.

Kerry Yo Nakagawa

Nakagawa Family

Kerry Yo Nakagawa's paternal grandfather, Hisataro Nakagawa, was born in Hiroshima, Japan, and came to the United States in 1886. He went first to ʻŌlaʻa, Hawaii, and eventually settled in Bowles, California, where he became a grape farmer. Kerry Yo's maternal grandfather, on the other hand, Matsutake Fukuda, immigrated to Seattle in 1895 and started a dairy farm in Auburn, Washington. One of his eleven children—Rosie— is Kerry Yo's mother. Toshio Tom Dyna Nakagawa was born in 1905, Kerry Yo's father. Both the Nakagawas and the Fukudas encountered multiple obstacles. Some were official, such as anti-immigration and anti-miscegenation laws, and the Alien Land Law. Matsutake Fukuda returned to Japan in 1933, and barely survived the atomic bomb that destroyed his house in 1945.

The Nakagawas were ordered to report to the Fresno Assembly Center after the war started, where they remained for six months. They were given only ten days to pack. Kerry Yo's parents and paternal grand-parents were sent to Jerome, Arkansas, while his maternal grandparents were assigned to Rohwer, Arkansas. Rosie Nakagawa recalls seeing signs from the train that stated things such as "Get out of Fresno" and "Never come back to California." The Japanese concepts of *gaman* and *gambaru*

Account provided by Kerry Yo Nakagawa (Sansei) from the conversations and oral histories with Yoshiko Rose Nakagawa and family. Story written by Julie Renee Moore (Sansei), Special Collections Research Center, Henry Madden Library, California State University, Fresno, for the exhibition "9066: Japanese American Voices from the Inside, 2017."

The Nakagawa family in 1942, in front of their Jerome, Arkansas, barrack, Block 41-40-A: Kerry Yo's mother Rose, father Dyna, and two-year-old sister Janie.

[to commit oneself fully to completing a challenging task] helped his family cope with their new lives in Arkansas. Toshio was head of the camp plumbing group, while Rosie raised a two-year-old daughter. Rosie's mother, Setsu, had told her while on the train to Jerome, "this is the greatest country in the world" and that "all have to pay a price for freedom." Setsu passed away in camp in 1943. Her body was cremated, and when Rosie opened the coffee can that her ashes were returned in, it contained a slip of paper that read "Jap Woman."

After the war the Nakagawas moved to Chicago, and three years later returned to California. Their neighbors, Jepp Raven and the McClurgs, had taken care of their property. They not only ran the farm, they gave Hisataro a cigar box full of the profits made over the years. Toshio resumed his work as a plumber in Fowler, and he and Rosie even opened a pool hall. Their daughter, Janie, worked for the Fowler School District for over forty years. Their son, Kerry Yo, found work in multimedia. His wife Jeri is a pharmacist, and their children, Kale and Jenna, work for Google in San Francisco and as an OB-GYN in Brooklyn, respectively. Kerry Yo and Jeri also have a two-year-old granddaughter, Olivia Rose (Osie).

Kerry Yo feels that Toshio and Rosie probably felt a sense of relief that the government admitted to imprisoning loyal Americans based solely on their race. They also believed that it was a land grab due to the amount of control Japanese Americans had over California's cash crops. Regarding the 1988 payments, according to Kerry Yo, "the $20,000 reparations were a token amount considering so many Issei never saw their checks, and how can one put a price on civil liberties, constitutional rights, homes, businesses, and dignities?"

Don Nakamoto

A Picture of My Mother

"Hey, look at this. Isn't this Grandma?" We had been looking at some of the exhibits at the Jerome-Rohwer Interpretive Museum and Visitors Center [now known as the World War II Japanese American Internment Museum] in McGehee, Arkansas, in 2015 when my daughter, in her early twenties, asked her question. She had been looking at a couple of ordinary white binders with a few pictures neatly stuffed into plastic page protectors. The binders were all that remained of any photographic records of the Jerome, Arkansas, internment camp since no internee cameras had been allowed in the Jerome camp, according to museum staff. There were many more pictures available from the Rohwer camp.

The fact that we were at this museum at all, viewing old camp pictures, had seemed highly improbable until just recently.

My daughter had landed her first full-time job as a TV news producer in Little Rock, Arkansas, roughly a two-hour drive from Jerome—my late mother (maiden name Matsuye Takeuchi) and father's (Nobuo Nakamoto) prison home during the war years. As Southern California residents, we had never envisioned visiting Jerome, but my daughter's new job opened the possibility of an exciting adventure.

After a little internet research, the idea of a visit lost some of its appeal. Jerome's population: thirty-five. No remaining remnants of the original internment camp. Not much to see, but there was a small two-room museum dedicated to the Rohwer and Jerome internment camps built inside an abandoned train station in nearby McGehee.

We debated whether to make the drive south into a borderline Deep South region we did not know. (A noted Ku Klux Klan gathering place was a couple hours' drive north of Little Rock.) My parents never said one word to me about their experience in the internment camps, so there wasn't much to relate to regarding Jerome or memorable experiences or insights about the camp.

We finally decided to go, more to see what the area of the camps was like rather than expecting to see anything of historical significance—and definitely with no expectation of seeing anything directly related to my parents.

The trip to Jerome seemed like an unending drive through green woods and farmland. Some relatives had talked about the swamps in the region, but we didn't see anything resembling a swamp. Some of the houses in the area looked like tiny shacks on stilts, and there weren't a lot of buildings or retail stores as we passed through Jerome. There indeed was no sign of a prison camp that once housed over eight thousand Japanese Americans.

We arrived at the red-brick internment museum in McGehee and viewed several exhibits with enlarged pictures of the interned Japanese Americans and information about the internment and the war.

Jerome, Arkansas

A Jerome resident, a local farmer probably in his late eighties or early nineties, was at the museum to talk to a children's book author. He said that most of the residents were against the creation of the museum prior to its opening in 2013. (George Takei, who was interned at nearby Rohwer, was the keynote speaker at the museum opening.) As a young boy, the farmer delivered vegetables to the camps and over the years became friends with some of the Japanese American boys in the camp. However, most of the people did not like having the camp in their area and did not like having the Japanese around, he said.

After viewing the museum exhibits, my daughter leafed through the binders, called me over, and asked if my mother was in a group picture. She had never met her grandmother and had only seen a few old pictures of her.

I looked at the picture, studied it closely, and nodded slightly. Yes, it was a picture of my mother sitting in the front row of a group of maybe 130 high school graduates, possibly the first high school graduating class in the camp. Graduating high school in the desolate swamplands of Arkansas behind barbed-wire fences must have been a bittersweet experience.

As we drove back to Little Rock, we pondered the improbability of ever seeing a picture of my mother among the few pictures that existed in such a faraway place. We considered the ironic sequence of events that led us to Jerome. We all concluded that my mother's spirit must have played some role in calling us back to her home during the war.

Tad Nakase

Wakayama, Japan

My father, Yoshio Kamon, also known as Kenichi Nakase, was born in Satono, Wakayama, Japan. He apprenticed and was trained as a carpenter/furniture maker. He immigrated to California via Mexico with his older brother Kazuo Kamon in the late 1930s.

My mother, Takayo Maeda, was born in the Coachella Valley of California. Her father and mother immigrated for farming opportunities in California. They had two sons and three daughters, all born in California. My mother's family moved back to Japan, and bought land to build a house and farm on a hill overlooking the ocean in Esumi, Wakayama, Japan; the house still exists. After attending school in Japan, my mother returned to California in 1938.

Executive Order 9066

My father and mother were married in Guadalupe, California, then a predominately Japanese American farming community located along the Central Coast of California. I was their first born. My mother was pregnant with my brother Gary when President Roosevelt signed Executive Order 9066, an order forcibly removing all Japanese, regardless of their citizenship, from the West Coast. My father was farming in an area called Oso Flaco, a few miles north of Guadalupe, an area that is still a rich farming area.

As a child during this time, I couldn't comprehend the impact of Executive Order 9066 on my family and the Japanese American community at large. Basic civil rights were violated; families, lives, businesses, communities were disrupted. With the future uncertain, my parents had to struggle with difficult decisions: What shall we take and what shall we leave? Where are they taking us? Will we be separated? Are they sending us to Japan? Where is the US government forcing us to go? How long will we be away? Money and time invested in the crop in the field, farm equipment and tools, furniture and personal items—to sell or store? Decisions regarding the future had to be made without knowing what the future held.

Santa Anita Assembly Center

My family was shipped to Santa Anita, a thoroughbred racing track located in Arcadia in the San Gabriel Valley east of Los Angeles, along with thousands of other Japanese Americans. We were housed in converted horse stables while the war relocation centers were being constructed.

Rohwer Relocation Center

In the fall of 1942, only my father and I were shipped by train with blackout windows to Rohwer Relocation Center, Desha County, Arkansas. My mother was near term with my younger brother, so she had to remain in Santa Anita. As a year-old baby, I was separated from my mother. This separation has had a long-lasting effect on me, even into adulthood.

I remember my father wearing a long black overcoat and a fedora hat as we waited to board the train. I'm sure he had his hands full traveling with me as a year-old baby, before disposable diapers and baby formula.

Life in Rohwer Relocation Center

After my mother gave birth to my brother, she came to Rohwer to join my father and me. During the time in Rohwer, my sister Carol and brother Roy came into our family. I remember finding a large bottle of orange soda. I hid it so that I could go back later to drink it alone. I got sick; I think it was orange concentrate. I was the youngest one in my group of friends; we would go to the mess hall kitchen just before dinner and try to get the *ko ge* [*okoge*], the overcooked brown rice that stuck to the rice pot. This was a treat for us. My father would take me fishing in the canals in the camp; this ignited in me a lifelong love for fishing.

War Is Over

We were released from the camp and took a long train ride back to California. We settled in Guadalupe. There was a lack of housing, so we stayed in a room in the back of the Buddhist church. Life was difficult for my parents. My mother and father both worked in the fields, supporting us. We later moved to Watsonville in Northern California where my father grew strawberries; my brother Steve was born during this time. Several years later we moved back to Central California, to Santa Maria, where my father again grew strawberries. My brother Frank was born during this time. I had a difficult time being away from my parents while being in school; I believe this anxiety was caused by being separated from my mother during the relocation process. From Santa Maria my parents decided to move the family to Whittier, California, where my father became a gardener to support our growing family. In Whittier my younger sister Susan was born. Education was a priority for my parents; all seven children graduated from college. My sister Carol became a schoolteacher, my brother Frank became a school psychologist, and my brother Gary and I started a wholesale nursery which is still an ongoing family business. Brother Steve became an accountant who, along with Gary and little sister Susan, now operates the nursery.

Alice Ichinaga Nanamura

You Have to Remember This Is from a Ten-Year-Old

When we heard that we were at war with Japan, we were worried. Being only nine, I really didn't know what to expect. Our family finally knew what was going on when we saw Japanese families transported to the Tulare County Fairgrounds. There were soldiers guarding the gates and perimeter of the grounds. We then knew we would be in the same position, but did not know where we were going. My school friends couldn't believe that something like this would take me away while the war was going on. They were mad at the government for doing this to us.

We left in the spring of 1942 to Fresno Assembly Center. Most of the families from Tulare were sent there also. I don't remember anything at all about that time. We then had to board a train that was going to take us further into the middle of the United States, but we didn't know where. All I can remember is that it was hot and the windows were covered by some black paper. I also got sick on the train, and to this day, I hate to go on a train anywhere.

We finally ended up in Jerome, Arkansas. There were barracks, barbwire, and soldiers with guns so that we knew that we would not get out anytime soon. All of our family was in one barrack, with Uncle John and Auntie Alice next to us, plus the kids. This is where we got acquainted with our relatives. I really didn't know them until that time, so some-

Reprinted with permission from May Takeda et al., *All We Could Carry: James K. & Kiyono Ichinaga's Children Remember the War Years (1941–46)* (self-pub., Pleasanton, CA: 2004).

thing good came out of that time. Uncle Henry used to carve birds from tree limbs and then paint them. He gave me two of them and I treasured them until I lost them somewhere. I never knew that there were so many Japanese people until we were in camp.

Alice Ichinaga Nanamura, 1944.

Another thing is that when Mom went to do laundry, we all had to help her carry the loads back and forth. Where she hung them, I don't know. When it rained, we had boards between the barracks to walk on to get to the middle of the block. The older men got together to play board games like checkers, cards, and go, or just sit around and reminisce about old times in California. Pop didn't have much time for these "bull sessions," but when he did, he just relaxed and enjoyed the companionship of the other detainees, since his job as head cook for our block was so stressful.

After the war was over, Dad got a job in Nebraska with a farmer who planted vegetables. All of us younger ones had to help harvest the crops. I can remember cabbage, onions, and potatoes. He then got a job in Sidney in an ordnance depot, and there David was born in 1945. While we were working for the farmer, one day while Dad was driving to work, I stood up behind the cab of the truck and Dad hit a bump in the road, and I fell backward off of the truck. I must have hit my head because that is why I sometimes can't remember some of the things that went on during this time. Bits and pieces come back to me at odd times. Okay, people, you can laugh and make jokes about this because I have already had comments about my state of mind, whatever it is!!!

At Sidney, Dad was in charge of some Italian war prisoners. They made a ship in a bottle and gave it to him. I remember it on the shelf of our house for a long time.

We came home in the spring of '45 and I was a freshman in high school. Boy, was it hard to adjust to being behind in some of my subjects. I really had a hard time and the friends that I had before I left made it easier to blend in and for me to be accepted again.

To finish up, all I can say is that Dad and Mom never gave up even though it was the bleakest time in their entire lives. We were very lucky to have them uplift all of us when it could have been worse.

We are all what they instilled in us: to do the best we can with what we have and had.

Alice Ichinaga Nanamura, 2000.

Joanne Y. Okada

As a child of five years of age, I hardly remember that much of having to leave our California home and going to the relocation camp. I do remember we left Santa Anita Assembly Center, Los Angeles. We boarded a train with soldiers standing and watching us with their weapons. We were on a one-way trip to Arkansas. The trip was very long, noisy, and crowded with other passengers like us. We were not allowed to look out the covered windows as we traveled through and around Arizona, New Mexico, Texas, and Oklahoma. We finally reached Arkansas, our destination, where we were met by more soldiers.

Camp days were hot, dusty, with windstorms and high humidity. We kids lived to get into the showers and cool off. That was our fun and play time. I recall the summers and the insect and mosquito bites that caused a terrible rash. It was unbearable at times. Winters were unlike the California weather we were used to.

My first day at school, first grade, I met my forever friend, Walter Imahara. I still have our class picture: we are sitting side by side. The next time I saw Walter was thirty-plus years later at a service in Utah. I had married and moved to Utah with my husband, Junior Okada. To see and recognize Walter immediately is still astonishing to me to this day. He had this unforgettable impish face! It is wonderful that we have kept in contact since then, and here we have come full circle to reconnect with our individual stories.

My return to California from camp was a period of adjustment. Grammar school was full of hostility, alone, not knowing anyone. Schoolmates were not kind. A group of Black American classmates came to my rescue and they became my friends and protectors. They made sure I was safe and taken care of. I will always be thankful and grateful to them.

I must make mention that the education we received in the

Above: Walter, first row, fourth from right (leaning); Joanne Okada, left of Walter.

Right: Joanne Okada (five years old) and her sister Janet Hayashi (nine years old) with Christmas dolls at Block 7 Barrack, Jerome, Arkansas; Christmas 1942.

internment camp was of the highest standard because we were able to fit easily into the curriculum of the school lessons. We were fortunate for that.

While at the same Theodore Roosevelt Grammar School, a student, Barbara Forbes Roebuck, befriended me right from the beginning. She and her family were Canadians and such kind, wonderful, caring people.

We rode our bikes, took piano lessons, and sang songs. This friendship extended straight through high school and even her college days when we she was attending California State University, Long Beach, and I was a secretary there. To this day, though she and her husband have passed, her children and grandchildren send Christmas cards.

Some things and lasting remembrances remain from those difficult, trying days of long ago.

Joanne Okada, 1983.

Lester Ouchida

Florin, California

My parents, Harold and Edith Ouchida, and five of us children, lived in Florin, California, prior to our internment. Florin, a small town south of Sacramento, had approximately 250 Japanese families living in the area. Most of the people had strawberry and grape farms. My father had a produce-shipping company by the time he was twenty-four years old and was doing very well.

My parents were both second-generation Nisei, high school graduates, and quite Americanized. Father played baseball for Elk Grove High School. They married in 1929 at ages twenty-four and nineteen and were thirty-seven and thirty-two, respectively, when Executive Order 9066 was issued in February 1942 and provided the authorization for internment. Their children were Kenneth (twelve at the time), Lucille (ten), Earl (eight), Lester (five), and Harold Jr. (two).

Assembly Center

On May 29, 1942, our family was sent to the San Joaquin County Fairgrounds in Stockton. This was one of many internment assembly centers to house one hundred twenty thousand Japanese from the states of Washington, Oregon, California, and Arizona prior to being sent to the ten permanent camps which were being built. Many families lived in horse stalls.

Jerome, Arkansas

In October 1942, our family was shipped by train to Jerome, Arkansas.

My father was a block manager and received a pay of $16 per month. The top pay for professionals like doctors was $19. Jerome was the first camp to be closed in June 1944, and our family was then relocated to Gila River, Arizona.

Seabrook Farms, New Jersey

So, we went from a swampland climate to that of a blistering heat. In 1944, my father was hired by Seabrook Farms in New Jersey to manage and to recruit Japanese Americans to work in this large agricultural center, as there was a vast shortage of labor due to the war. Approximately three thousand Japanese Americans were hired by Seabrook.

Florin, California

In August 1945, we returned to Florin by Greyhound bus. I can still remember the ladies on the bus crying as we stopped to make a turn onto Florin Road. They were home after 3½ years.

My father resumed his produce-delivery business, but it did not achieve the prosperity of the prewar years. Many of the Japanese had lost their homes and farms. We had a good neighbor, Mary McComber, who rented our house for us. We fortunately had a house to return to. There were other individuals and groups, such as the Quakers, who helped the Japanese. I was fortunate in being young and unaware of the world outside the internment camps. My oldest brother said he did not at all enjoy the camp life . . . he lost high school years.

I attended the "Life Interrupted" reunion and remembrance of Jerome and Rohwer in Arkansas in September 2004. It was a memorable gathering of over 1,300 people. President Clinton was to be the keynote speaker but had to cancel because of surgery. Senator Daniel Inouye spoke, and I remember his story of returning after the war and walking into a barber shop with his full Army uniform, chest full of battle ribbons, and a missing arm. He was refused a haircut because he was a "Jap." A Medal of Honor recipient was denied a haircut.

I am eighty-two years old, but I've always had an interest in the internment and the World War II years. I'm very proud of how our Nisei parents conducted themselves. I am also very proud of the Nisei boys who volunteered to fight for our country in spite of how our country was treating their families.

442nd Regimental Combat Team

The segregated Japanese American 442nd Regimental Combat Team became the most decorated unit of its size and length of service in the history of the US Army. They received twenty-one Medals of Honor and over 9,400 Purple Hearts. There were others that refused to join the military because they felt strongly about the internment being a violation of their constitutional rights. They were also taking a courageous stand. A lesser-known story is that over six thousand Nisei served in the Pacific Theater of WWII under General MacArthur and were invaluable in saving lives on both sides and in shortening the war.

Memorial listing Medal of Honor recipients at the "Go for Broke" Monument in Los Angeles, California. *Photo: Walter Imahara.*

I volunteer as a docent at the California State Museum and tell mostly schoolchildren about the internment experience. I tell them about President Carter setting up a commission to study why our country interned Japanese Americans. The commission concluded that it happened for three reasons—racism, war hysteria, and lack of political leadership—and recommended an apology and reparations. This resulted in the redress legislation—the Civil Liberties Act of 1987. A Harvard University case study (C-16-90-1006.0), *Against All Odds*, provides an excellent write-up on the campaign for redress.

In conclusion, what harm did Japanese Americans do to suffer for three years of internment? We lost our freedom and privacy, we lost financially, and we lost some degree of self-respect. However, I believe that the perseverance, integrity, and courage of our parents and Nisei boys as well as the continuing attitude of Japanese Americans has gained us the respect of our country.

Lastly, a seven-part documentary video has been completed by a friend, Catherine Busch, which may be accessed at www.wethepeople series.com. She grew up in Pennsylvania and learned later in life about the internment. She was incensed about this and developed a passion to create a comprehensive, lasting educational video on the internment and its ramifications and aftereffects. The seven parts of the video series are:

1. Uprooted
2. Incarceration
3. Go for Broke (The 442nd Regiment)
4. Returning Home
5. Those Who Helped
6. Racism and Redress
7. Could It Happen Again?

You can access this entire video at https://wethepeopleseries.com/.

Ellen Kazuko Hachiya Oye

Remembrance of Life in Jerome, Arkansas

The Hachiya family was relocated from Long Beach, California, to Jerome, Arkansas, after initial roundup (word not used lightly) to Santa Anita stables in California. Presumably, Santa Anita was intended to be a temporary location prior to assignment to more habitable (?) living quarters in designated remote areas throughout various regions of the US.

The family, in addition to parents Eiichi Henry and Yoshiko Hachiya, both born in the US, included their three eldest children, Ellen Kazuko, Donald Takeshi, and James Shoji. The last three children were born in relocation camps—Kenji in November 1942 and Kiyoshi in January 1944 in Jerome, and Mitsuye in June 1945 in Heart Mountain, Wyoming.

Although brother Kiyoshi always lists Jerome, Arkansas, as his birthplace whenever asked, he was informed by someone during his high school years, or just prior to his enlistment in the US Army, that there was no place called "Jerome." In attempting to verify his birthplace, he discovered that his birth certificate lists Denson, Arkansas, as his birthplace.

Being only four years old living in Jerome, memories are truly nonexistent to be able to write a substantial report of any kind. The main purpose of submitting this very short personal essay is aimed at being listed as internee for historical reasons. The family was reassigned to the Heart Mountain, Wyoming, relocation camp in 1944 just prior to release, and at the end of the war in 1945, back to Long Beach, California.

Life for all internees was very sad and depressing. However, returning to Long Beach from segregated living areas of a 100 percent Japanese population did not prepare this writer for all the prejudices and hatred faced in the outside world. Attending schools and living in government-provided trailer courts was a dark period for this writer— surprisingly much worse than living in the camps. Remembering the outward prejudices and perceived hatred still affects this writer to this day some seventy-plus years later.

Tamio Tom Sakurai

Life on a truck farm in Carson (now part of Torrance), California, for a six-year-old in 1941 was one of seeking an adventure each day. Living with only my parents, and the nearest neighbor being way beyond my parental boundary, forced me to investigate the land and barn for small animals or into pretending to be a cowboy, pilot, or whatever and wherever my imagination took me. I was always the hero.

December 7, 1941

Then on December 7, the Japanese bombed Pearl Harbor and my life took an abrupt turn. Mr. Nakamura, our nearest neighbor, came running breathlessly up the hill to our home, plopping himself on our porch. While fanning himself with his hat he spoke rapidly in Japanese, taking deep breaths between sentences, telling my parents of the Pearl Harbor bombing. My parents were unaware of the bombing because we did not have a radio or telephone. At that time, the radio was the most immediate way most people received the news. The Japanese newspaper, delivered a few days later for rural subscribers, reported the bombing and destruction that took place. My parents were incredulous and couldn't believe what had happened.

Mr. Nakamura and my parents talked about the possibility of being taken to jail. My mother kept saying, "What should we do?" They quickly started cutting figures of relatives or friends wearing Japanese military uniform out of photos, and burning them along with any Japanese artifacts they thought might be incriminating. My uncle rushed over, too, and he and my dad huddled together and, after an intense discussion, decided

The story of Tamio Tom Sakurai as told to Amy Iwamasa, his neighbor.

what to do with important objects, documents, and cash they had on hand. Together they decided to put those items in a bottle and bury it in cement below our wood frame house. The cache remained there until we returned after the war to retrieve it. To my parents' dismay, pig farmers used the house to shelter and raise their pigs. It was destroyed.

Soon after the bombing of Pearl Harbor, FBI agents visited my grandfather and arrested him because he was affiliated with the Compton Gauken Japanese School. He was taken to a holding center in Tujunga Canyon, California, and joined by many other Japanese community leaders who were abruptly taken from their homes and imprisoned. Grandfather was later reunited with us in Jerome, Arkansas. My grandmother had passed away in 1939 so was not involved in the internment experience.

How my parents received notification to evacuate and assemble at the Santa Anita racetrack is unknown to me. Rushing from room to room, my mother gathered essential items and packed a suitcase for me. She was packing for the unknown future and wanted to ensure we were prepared for every need. As she handled items, she took a deep breath and made a decision of leaving or taking a book or toy, a necessity or not. Later, when dances were held at Santa Anita, I recalled seeing women dressed in fancy kimonos and dresses and thinking they must have had more than one suitcase. Why did they have such fancy clothes? That was not an important or necessary item. Did they not follow the orders?

Santa Anita Assembly Center

A bus took us to the Santa Anita racetrack near Los Angeles. As I stepped off the bus, I vividly remember the smell of the horse stables, and that afternoon making a mattress with hay. But being six years old, I was quickly occupied with running to the pond in the racetrack infield and catching pollywogs. Those play days were limited because I was sick so often. I recall the home remedy of mustard plaster that my mother smeared on my chest, and the newspaper she wrapped around my torso to retain the heat of the mustard plaster. Finally, we were moved to temporary barracks constructed in the parking lot. They were small but better than the horse stable. Shortly after our arrival, a school setting in the grandstand was started. The teachers, mostly Japanese, conducted lessons orally because regular school texts and supplies were unavailable. So, the students learned their subjects through oral and rote memory instruction.

Eating in the mess hall, cafeteria style, with other families was not an environment that my parents felt was conducive to family life. So, my mother went to the mess hall every day for every meal and brought it home for my dad and me. As days slipped by, life became a challenge and I wanted to explore my environment. I would sneak off and go to various mess halls identified by color. Everyone was assigned a color and could not cross over to other mess halls. I could not resist the lure of finding out the truth of "camp talk," so I would venture to other mess halls based upon gossip of better food being served. But in the end, everyone agreed the food was lousy.

Jerome Internment Camp, Arkansas

One day we were loaded on a train and headed east. The curtains were drawn so we did not see the landscape as the train moved toward its destination, what we later found out to be Jerome, Arkansas. A frightening incident occurred: the train came to a full stop by a deep gorge. People started asking why the train was stopped at that spot. Other people shouted out, "They are going to toss us out of the train into the gorge!" Then people started getting panicky and the older adults started burning *senko* (incense), praying and crying. There was shouting and total chaos until the train started up again and crossed the bridge. This incident remains vivid in my mind even after all these years have passed.

It took about five days to reach Jerome. The weather was chilly and cold, wet and damp on the day of our arrival. When we looked out the bus/train window, we could see the rows upon rows of barracks. A canal encircled the camp, which was used to drain water that pooled on the campground. At the assembly area, we were assigned a barrack, Block 3 —Barrack 5B or 3/5B. Our neighbors were the Yoshidas and Okas.

Once we were settled, I took off to explore the canal and discovered the snapping turtles that I found irresistible, and proceeded to agitate them with a stick. As we got older and more familiar with the terrain, some of the boys on the block would go into the woods to trap rabbits or small animals. As kids with limited or no play equipment, we would play simple games that required no equipment and were spontaneous, games such as "kick the can," "hide and go seek," and "Annie, Annie Over." My dad was a projectionist and so I was able to see a movie every night, and my favorites that I saw over and over again were *Meet Me in St. Louis* starring Judy Garland and Mickey Rooney, and *Thirty Seconds over Tokyo* featuring Spencer Tracy and Van Johnson.

Rohwer Relocation Center

As I was told, we were moved to Rohwer because German POWs (prisoners of war) were going to be imprisoned in Jerome. We couldn't understand why? But we figured that because Jerome was so desolate, there was nowhere for the imprisoned soldiers to go without being recognized. They were treated well, housed well, and ate well.

My recollection of Rohwer is very limited. There seemed to be little difference in daily life from Jerome to Rohwer for a six-year-old. But I do recall that mothers of sons going off to the military or war would go barrack to barrack, asking for the occupants to sew a stitch on a *sennin bari* (a cloth cummerbund); "a thousand stitches, a thousand people hoping for your safe return," the mothers would say.

My dad, being a lumberjack and working in a warehouse, had contact with local drivers who came to deliver supplies. It was through these interactions that he realized that many were illiterate. In the town of McGehee, the newspaper was read aloud to the men gathered around a potbelly stove. This, in his mind, further validated his beliefs that many of the locals were not well educated. He then took advantage of the situation and falsified the warehouse orders, and used the supplies to consume or sell in the black market.

My mother had more time on her hands; therefore, she was still planning for my future. The war could not go on forever. They were going to go back to Japan, and she did not want me to be illiterate. Therefore, she copied a Japanese school text borrowed from a neighbor and copied every character on each page, and even drew the pictures used to illustrate the learning concepts. Using that book she so diligently reproduced, she taught me Japanese. Years later, when I was in the army stationed in New Jersey, I wrote her letters in Japanese and she was so proud of me. She saved every letter and would share them with her friends, and said all her work proved fruitful. "Now I can communicate with my son," she said. And I still have and cherish the book that my mother so lovingly put together for me so many years ago.

Everyone had time on their hands. My dad collected pieces of swamp wood and brought them home carefully, inspecting them for shape, grain, and beauty of the wood. Then he would sand and polish them until they gleamed in the light. He made a walking cane that he really cherished because of its knotty and snarled shape. It remains with our family as a symbol of days incarcerated during WWII. Each time we handle it and trace our hands over and follow its irregular shape, memories of those long-ago days become vivid.

War Was Over 1945

The war ended in 1945 after the Japanese surrendered. I was ten years old and again packed and got ready to travel. We were waiting outside Rohwer, ready to board the bus. Okasan (mother) wore her traveling clothes: a nice dress, a worn coat, black heavy shoes, and a hat with netting hanging down and surrounding her face. Finally, the bus came to pick us up at the gate, and we picked up our luggage and started walking toward the bus. Suddenly, Okasan turned around and took a deep breath and brought up spit and anger from deep within her, and faced the campground. She let it out but, to her disgust, the spit went no further than the netting and back on her face. As a kid, I laughed. I was on my way to another adventure to Chicago to stay with an aunt, and then on to Cleveland before returning to Southern California.

Rose Futamachi Sasaki

Stockton Assembly Center

I was eight years old when my parents and six-year-old sister and four-year-old brother were ordered from our home in Terminus, California, and into the Stockton Assembly Center. At the time, my father was supervising a three-thousand-acre ranch for Atkin Kroll & Co. in San Francisco. After the attack on Pearl Harbor, all Japanese on the West Coast were under suspicion, and the FBI began a house-to-house search of Japanese homes looking for anything linked to Japan. To avoid arrest, people burned or destroyed anything Japanese. Father tossed his swords and guns down a well, and other objects onto a bonfire. I remember how sad I was seeing my Japanese dolls thrown into the fire.

In May 1942, we were driven by truck with other families to the San Joaquin County Fairground and assigned to live in Block 1, Barrack 2, Apartment A. Luckily, it was near the entrance to the fairground so it was landscaped with a row of trees and a fountain, but the mess hall was far away. I finished third grade in the assembly center. I remember that we considered the principal, Mr. Takeuchi, mean and scary because he would spank students who were bad. After school, my classmate Paul Sakamoto and I liked to catch blue-bellied lizards.

Rohwer Relocation Center

After seven months at the Stockton Assembly Center, we were ordered to carry our own suitcases and walk a mile down Charter Way to the train depot. The old train had hard bench seats and we weren't allowed to pull up the shades. At night, my father would stack our suitcases between the two benches, so we could recline a bit. It took five days to reach our relocation center in Rohwer, Arkansas. We lived on Block 19, Barrack 4, Apartment A. We moved to 19-4-F after the Hirokane family got transferred to Tule Lake, because that space was larger and closer to the washroom and mess hall.

Unlike California, Arkansas was hot and humid in the summer and bitter cold and snowy in the winter. On icy days, my uncle, Lloyd Shingu, would put on his spiked golf shoes and lead me, my sister, and cousins hand-in-hand to school to keep us from sliding into the deep ditches. My father, Harry Futamachi, had a job in the police department and after his shift ended, he would detour past the coal pile and "pocket" a few lumps to add heat to our potbelly stove. I liked to put a cup of chocolate milk on the ledge inside our apartment so it would freeze into a popsicle by morning.

I started fourth grade at Rohwer, with Miss Hayes as my teacher and Kiichi Hiramoto as the teacher's aide. I'd walk to school with my block friends, and on the way, we would hunt for wild *hozuki* berries in the woods. We'd pop out the seed and chomp on the hollow berry to make frog-like sounds. I was in the Brownies with Miss Avery as leader, and learned tap-dance routines from Doris Ito for the block Christmas party. Father attached taps to my saddle shoes. The kids I played with in camp became lifelong friends.

After Rohwer

When the WRA announced that the camps would be closed and we were free to leave, my father learned that he and the Japanese work crew under his charge would not be hired back. With anti-Japanese hostility making housing and jobs scarce on the West Coast, my father and his brother-in-law, Lloyd Shingu, decided to explore opportunities in the South. To deflect anti-Japanese reactions, they assumed Chinese-sounding names. Instead of Futamachi, my father called himself Mr. Fu, and Uncle Lloyd went by Mr. Shin. In the end, they accepted a sharecropping offer from a landowner named Virginia Brown in Scott, Arkansas. We moved to Scott with five other families from Rohwer—Shingu, Nakamura, Yada, Yoshimura, and Oshima—and were housed in former slave quarters that had a corrugated tin roof, with no electricity or running water. The men set about growing tomatoes, okra, eggplant, beans, spinach, cantaloupe, and corn, which they sold to local produce buyers. These were crops that required irrigation, a practice unknown in the South, which mostly raised dry-farmed cotton. My father's method of irrigation farming was viewed as so revolutionary that Arkansas newspapers even wrote about it. Meanwhile, my siblings and I attended the local schools. The schools were segregated into all-Black and all-white schools, leaving us unsure where we belonged. Our landlord settled it by demanding that we be allowed into the white school. We got a mostly friendly reception from classmates and I still keep in touch with some. But in 1949, my father died, and my uncle in Cincinnati insisted that we move in with him. We lived in Cincinnati for a year and finally moved back to California, where my mother's uncle and aunt found us a place to stay in Stockton. Finally, we were able to reconnect with the life we knew before camp.

Joh Sekiguchi

The Bread Sheet

Many people in our area remember Mrs. Nomura for her cooking skills. Mrs. Nomura was short and round and made amazing fried noodles. She and her daughter, Emily, ran Lindsay Chop Suey—a Chinese restaurant in Lindsay, California. It was known for its generous portions. One friend, who ate there years ago, says she has never been able to find sauces that tasted as good at any other Chinese restaurant—cheap or expensive. The restaurant was in an old, wooden, two-story building that began to lean as the decades went by. I remember when there was a wooden or board sidewalk out front. Maybe there was a hitching post at one time. Mrs. Nomura lived to be over one hundred years old. A few years ago, my Uncle Joh recalled this story and shared it with me. —CLOVER JOHNSON

My mother was good friends with Mrs. Nomura. My family (the Sekiguchi family) and the Nomura family lived in Lindsay before the war and we all ended up in the Jerome Relocation Center together. The Nagatas from Tulare went there, too.

The meals at the Jerome center were not great—often greasy or starchy or calorie dense. I was a growing boy, so it didn't bother me too much; we got breakfast, lunch, and dinner every day. I remember having scrambled eggs and stewed prunes for breakfast. There was fresh cantaloupe after people started growing melons. The farmers who got together

As told to Clover Johnson by Joh Sekiguchi (1930–2020).

124

One of the Jerome Relocation Center dining halls that had been decorated for a special occasion.

and cleared some land were eventually able to provide fresh vegetables for the camp. My mother worked as a cook's helper in one of the camp's mess halls. There was a dietician for the entire camp who was authorized to come up with the menus for all the kitchens, so our food was supposed to be balanced and nutritious. As I recall, there was this load of very scrawny—not Grade A—chickens that arrived . . . I was told we got what the NCOs in the Army were eating. There was a lot of chipped beef and white bread. I wished we'd had wheat bread, but as a kid I could have all the white bread and peanut butter and apple butter I wanted.

The Jerome camp had been built in a swampy area. In the summer it was very hot and muggy. Not bad for growing vegetables—or mosquitoes. While I was eating dinner in the mess hall, there would be a black cloud of mosquitoes waiting for me outside. I would have to run from one place to another to try and keep away from them. There was one small plus to living in a camp in Arkansas—on occasion we did get seafood, like shrimp and oysters, from the Gulf.

Well, my mother's friend, Mrs. Nomura, hoarded food. It wasn't uncommon for people to take a little bread back to their living quarters to eat later, maybe as a bedtime snack. Mrs. Nomura took bread from the dining hall and dried it out to save. I am not sure why. Perhaps she was worried that her family would go hungry in the future. Eventually she had a whole sheet full of dried bread in her family quarters. The Jerome center was the first center to close, so we all had to pack up and go someplace else. Mrs. Nomura left her large bundle behind when everyone went to the next camp. I wonder what the people who found it thought.

Sharp Park

Our father, Nobara Kumakichi Sekiguchi, had an encounter with the FBI when I was about four or five years old. My family was living in the Huntington Beach area of Southern California at the time. Dad had a job teaching at the Talbert Japanese language school. Well, someone accused our dad of being a communist. The Great Depression was going on and people were looking for answers. Things were difficult and some folks wondered if communism could make their lives better. Not everyone wanted communism to spread; government men came in a big, black, 1934 Ford V-8 to question Dad. They wore black—one came to the back door of the house. I saw a man in a black suit out front, too. They took Dad in and asked him if he was a communist. He was later released after convincing them that he was not. Our father just enjoyed studying and discussing all types of religions and philosophies and popular ideas.

When our mother's father became ill, our whole family went to Japan to see him. Fortunately, he recovered. At the end of our stay in Japan, we left my older sister, Suzuko, there to go to school. My parents and my younger sister and I returned to America. Dad had gotten a job teaching Japanese in Lindsay, California.

We were living in Lindsay when Japan bombed Pearl Harbor in December of 1941. Not very long after that, the police came to the "Gakko" or Japanese language school to get our father. They told him to pack a suitcase—to take his shaving kit and a towel. This time Dad didn't come right home. From Lindsay, he was taken to the jail in Visalia. After that he was taken to Sharp Park, south of San Francisco, where he was interrogated. (Sharp Park was first a golf course, and then a relief camp before it became an Immigration and Naturalization Service temporary holding station for enemy aliens on March 30, 1942. Japanese, Italian, and German men were held there.)

I don't know if there were others from the Lindsay area or not, but like our father, many other Japanese men were just taken from their homes and sent to Sharp Park. At the time, there were individuals who "tattled," pointing out to the authorities the kind of people the FBI was looking for—Issei (first-generation Japanese) who were influential or were community leaders or had ties to Japan or who might have been considered a threat. Among these were Buddhist/Shinto priests, doctors, teachers, ministers, those involved in media (journalists, photographers, and newspaper reporters), Japanese-language schoolteachers, martial arts instructors, those involved in the import/export business, those who owned fishing boats. . . . Maybe the "tattlers" wanted to look like loyal American citizens by cooperating. Maybe they were just afraid not to. Either way, that kind of information was no secret and the authorities could have easily found it out on their own.

After our father was taken, our mother cried every day. She didn't know when—or if—he would be coming back. She didn't know what would happen to our sister Suzuko in Japan. She had no job of her own and no way to earn money. When the money she had left ran out, she didn't know how she would put food on the table for my younger sister, Mariko, and me. In a way, it was a relief to our mother when we were ordered to go to the Fresno Assembly Center in May of 1942. At the assembly center she didn't have to worry about keeping us from going hungry.

Some of the local Lindsay church ladies felt very sorry for our family. They wrote letters to the authorities on our father's behalf to vouch for his character. It was eventually decided that he was harmless, and he was released to join the three of us at the Fresno Assembly Center. Others were released, too, but not all the Japanese men who were at Sharp Park with our father were allowed to return to their friends and families. Some were sent to the Tule Lake Relocation Center in Northern California and some went back to Japan on a prisoner exchange ship. Others were taken to the Department of Justice camps like Santa Fe, New Mexico, or to Army facilities.

Skinny-Dipping in the Mississippi

While I was working at Northrop, I made friends with a fellow engineer named Jimmy Jones. Jimmy is African American, and I am Japanese American, but we have one unique thing in common: boyhood memories of life in Arkansas. We both remember fishing in the creeks, catching huge catfish, and fighting off swarms of hungry mosquitoes that bred in the swamps. Jimmy came from a small town that was south of Jerome, Arkansas, where the "camp" or relocation center that my family was sent to during WWII was located. His family was dirt poor and he grew up

The Sekiguchi family: Joh, his father Nobara K., older sister Suzuko (back), younger sister Mariko (front), and mother, Tadako.

eating chitlins and turnip greens. By studying hard—getting an education—Jimmy was able to become an engineer and afford a comfortable life in Southern California. Still, he never forgot his home, and about every year or so Jimmy would return to Arkansas to visit his family. He occasionally offered to take me back with him, but I never took him up on it.

Ten years have gone by since I last talked with Jimmy. I've thought about looking him up and telling him that I finally made that trip. Earlier this year I went with a group of former detainees to Arkansas to visit the site of the Jerome Relocation Center. Now there is a huge farm where the camp once stood. Nothing remains but the towering chimney that was once part of the hospital incinerator. I remember that chimney well. Both of my parents had jobs at the hospital, and they'd aim for it as they walked across the camp from our "apartment" to work.

Besides the chimney, today there is only a memorial marker to indicate that this was the former location of the center. At the site I found nothing else. No abandoned cemetery. No concrete foundations. No overgrown roads. Nothing left to search for on the ground. I scanned the terrain and found nothing recognizable. The land itself has become featureless—the high spots and gullies smoothed flat and the swamps drained. I remember that there had been wooded areas containing an abundance of birds and other fauna. It would have been nice to again see the things that had interested me as a boy such as flying squirrels, poisonous snakes, and bizarre fish trapped in shallow ponds.

Originally the Jerome Relocation Center had been built on very cheap government land—land that had been inhospitable and practically useless. I was a twelve-year-old boy when I arrived in Arkansas for the first time. To my friends and me, the surrounding woods and swamps provided endless hours of entertainment. We were mean boys, beating rabbits out of the brush with sticks and chasing them until they were exhausted. They'd eventually just huddle there, quivering with fright and unable to move another inch.

Besides hunting rabbits, we liked to fish. There were bayous, small creeks, and shallow ponds with a variety of fish—some quite large, others so strange they seemed to have belonged on another planet. I remember catching fish and taking them back to camp to eat, thinking fresh fish would be a welcome change from the usual fare. Well, those fish weren't inedible, but the problem was they didn't have any flavor at all.

A family friend stands in front of the hospital-incinerator chimney, a prominent camp feature that was hard to miss.

Exploring the outdoors was far more exciting than attending classes—especially when the temperature rose. Because of moving—first to assembly centers and then to Jerome—my classmates and I had lost a lot of time from school. It was decided that we had to attend classes over the summer to make up the work we'd missed. There was no air conditioning back then. The Arkansas humidity made studying in the heat even more unbearable. I recall sweating so much that if my hand touched my paper it would become too soaked to write on anymore. Often there were terrible thunderstorms—not like anything I'd experienced in California.

All that humidity and rain did help keep the area green and lush. This reminded my mother of Japan. She also enjoyed the fireflies and the vibrant colors that came with the changing seasons. But that humidity was especially hard on people who had health problems like tuberculosis. One of my mother's friends became seriously ill with that disease; she died in the camp hospital.

Despite the hardships, the adults tried to make life as normal as possible for us kids. Baseball was popular in the camps. From time to time there were various forms of entertainment: music, plays, even sumo matches. We also had scouting in Arkansas. In 1943 they even

Joh Sekiguchi and his sister Mariko paying attention to a lesson taught by their father, Nobara K. Sekiguchi.

held a Boy Scout jamboree. The scouts from the two relocation camps, Jerome and Rohwer, were loaded into the back of supply trucks and rode into town. There we were joined by the local scouts from Arkansas City. I remember one boy climbing in with the rest of us and I noticed other boys from town in the other trucks. It must have taken a lot of courage for them to join a bunch of complete strangers—especially strangers many folks considered to be "the enemy." Some of the boys from the relocation centers had brought their scout uniforms with them when they relocated, but none of the Arkansas City boys had uniforms.

We all gathered on the banks of the Mississippi River and set up camps. Our shelter covers were made from poles and olive-green army blankets, and we slept on army cots. I think the town scouts slept on the ground. Our breakfast was powdered eggs and hot cereal. Lunch and dinner were trucked in from the relocation centers. It was like army food: calorie dense, gooey, and filling, but it did include a dessert. A friend and I snuck over into the Arkansas City scouts' area to see what they were eating. They had one huge pot of beans with some chunks of fat floating in it. The Arkansas scouts got one bowl each, for which they seemed grateful.

One of the jamboree activities was swimming. The river was very muddy, and tiny red shrimp-like critters would bite you if you didn't keep moving. That wasn't much fun for me. Those Arkansas City boys didn't seem to mind as they stripped off their clothes and went skinny-dipping in the Mississippi. They whooped and hollered, not caring who was watching them splashing naked in the water.

Besides swimming, we also passed the time watching the paddle steamboats. They went upstream so slowly that they hardly seemed to be making any progress at all. They went downstream a whole lot faster. At night the boats would be all lit up. There was music and partying on board. People were laughing and acting carefree as if there wasn't a war going on.

The jamboree also included lots of singing. I still remember the "1,000-verse" song that the Arkansas City boys taught us. It went like this:

"I love Maggie, you love Maggie, we all love Maggie Darling. Second verse, same as the first, same tune, same words, I love Maggie, you love Maggie, we all love Maggie Darling. . . ."

We sang and laughed together with the Arkansas City scouts around a campfire on the banks of the Mississippi. A lot of people must have worked very hard just to give us that opportunity. That was the one and only jamboree our three scout troops got to enjoy together. The Jerome camp closed before we got to have another, and my family was moved to a relocation center in Arizona.

It's been over sixty years since I camped near the banks of the Mississippi River. I wonder if Boy Scouts in that part of the South are still skinny-dipping in the muddy water and singing the "Maggie" song as they watch the riverboats drift downstream.

My Uncle Joh went with a group to visit the Jerome camp site many years ago before the monuments and signs were put up and the museum was built. He is now in his late eighties, so it has been a very long time since that Boy Scout jamboree. He still remembers. —CLOVER JOHNSON

Fred Shimasaki

Strathmore, California, 1941

Prior to internment, my family lived and worked on a farm in Strathmore in Central California. The town was small, quiet, and mostly grape, olive, and orange groves. My father grew grapes, persimmons, and figs on a plot of land owned by his boss Mr. Crawford. In the fall, my brother Sam and I picked grapes and put them on trays to make raisins. We were paid per tray and made enough to buy football shoes for the season. I lived with my parents, two sisters, and four of my five brothers. My father passed in February of 1941 from lung cancer.

My oldest brother Tom lived on another farm nearby, north of Lindsay, California, which is where I was, picking peas, on December 7. I came in at lunchtime and heard the devastating news that Japan had bombed Pearl Harbor. The next day the bus ride to school was a very quiet ride. Usually, everyone yells and sings songs, but for the first time it was silent. When we got to school the principal explained what had happened, and that we (the Japanese American students) were Americans like everyone else and should be treated as such.

I was eighteen years old when I left for camp. I didn't quite graduate Strathmore High School, but the principal said to consider myself graduated even though I didn't take my final exams. My Caucasian friends said they wished they were Japanese so they could graduate without taking their final exams, too.

Jerome, Arkansas

When we left home for the Fresno Assembly Center, I cried. It was very sad for me. There we lived in a horse stall until we traveled by train to Jerome, in the swamplands of Arkansas. We ended up at the same camp as my dad's brother's family, the Idetas. My brother Sam and I became close to my cousins Tak and Chuck, playing bridge with them almost every evening.

In the winter, it rained a lot. In the summer, it was hot. People in camp got sunburned and turned brown. I worked in the carpentry shop Monday to Friday. I cut wood for individual customers who would make furniture for their barracks. Some would insist on using the power saws themselves and nick their fingers. I always told them, you better let me do it for you instead. Carpentry work paid $16 a month. One day working as a carpenter at the camp hospital, a lady there said she needed blood donors. I said, well, I'll donate blood if you give me a steak dinner. She was desperate, so she said yes. I donated blood a few more times for a steak dinner.

On our weekends off, we were required to go into the forest to chop down firewood since we didn't have the luxury of coal for fuel at camp. We chopped trees to about six-foot logs and took them back to camp. Ladies would take two-handed saws and cut those logs into twelve- to eighteen-inch logs. Those chopped into two halves would fit into our stoves. My brother Sam and I would wheelbarrow the cut firewood to the doorsteps of other families without men, so the women wouldn't have to go to the middle of camp to get a few themselves. Our block manager, who was Hawaiian, gave the block of Hawaiian families our firewood. It was irritating.

A Caucasian friend from back home in Lindsay, California, Paul Strate, was in the army in Texas and took part of his leave to visit me for a few days in camp. He ate meals with us in the mess hall, but one evening we had squid. He couldn't stomach it, so my mother brought him a peanut butter sandwich from the kitchen. My mother worked in the kitchens in camp for eight-hour days, five days a week. Back on the farm, she used to work twelve-hour days with no days off. In camp, she had time for hobbies like knitting and attending church. This is the one thing I appreciated about concentration camp: my mother didn't have to work as hard as she did on the farm.

I still remember the day my niece Janet was born in our barracks. Our barrack was partitioned with wooden frames and plastic into three rooms, each sleeping three or four, but the partitions didn't reach the ceilings. My sister-in-law Mitsuye was screaming loud. My brother Tom went to the hospital to get an ambulance to come, but it was too late. My mother helped Mitsuye with the birth.

Word got around about a "loyalty survey" issued by the government to all the men in camp that were seventeen and older. We knew its two questions before taking it: Would we be loyal to the USA? And would we fight for our country? I said Yes-Yes, though before, when talking about the draft came around, my mom discouraged me and my three of-age brothers from volunteering. She said only to go if drafted. I said Yes-Yes because I was born in America and despite the discrimination, I enjoyed the many things our country had to offer. Plus, I had many friends here. A few guys volunteered to go to the army at camp but had to leave in the middle of the night to avoid confrontation and injury. A group of people at camp were very antagonistic to those who joined the army.

Monroe, Michigan

Since I answered Yes-Yes, I could leave camp for work. One spring, until December, I left for Greening Nursery in Monroe, Michigan. It was the first time I had traveled somewhere alone. Monroe was half Italian and half French. An Italian guy who saw me said, "You, Japanese; me, Italiano," and gave me a fascist salute. I felt at that point that the government got things wrong and sent the wrong people to camp.

My brother Ira also left camp and worked with me at Greening, but I became friends with another guy around my age from Jerome named Kiyo Renge. We budded peach trees and did other hard work for fifty cents an hour. I went to work in Michigan because I felt like I was stagnating in camp. I remember another guy left camp for work at Greening because he was avoiding a gal he had sex with who wanted to marry him. We all had our reasons for leaving.

The Army

When I was drafted from Rohwer, I went to Camp Wheeler in Georgia for training, but came back. The Red Cross told me and my brothers Sam and Ira to visit my mother before going overseas with the 442nd because she had come down with cancer. My mom had symptoms of cancer in her stomach, but the doctors there didn't diagnose it right away, so it got bad before they finally realized. Even after, the doctors there didn't really know how to treat cancer because they were general practitioners and not specialists. They eventually moved my mom to Tooele, Utah, for better care. I remember during our visit to camp, my mom said to take a family picture since my brothers and I were back together with the family. My oldest brother Tom finally got all the kids together for the picture, but excluded my mom from it. It might be because she was very sick at the time. When my brothers and I went back to the army, the 442nd had already left for Europe.

By the time I left for Europe with the army, the war was over. I was stationed in Liège, Belgium, with the 390th MP Battalion and ordered to guard freight trains. Most of the time, hungry civilians would try and loot the trains for food. We would get on the ten-car trains and ride the same route to Antwerp, Belgium, then to Cologne, Germany, and down the Rhine River. At the end of our route at the relief station, kids would sell us German booze, which we called potato schnapps, and we'd get drunk off it.

Back to California

When my service finished, I went back to Lindsay, California, to stay with my oldest brother Tom and his family. Tom leased his farm for free to the Mexicans while we were gone at camp. When we came back, we grew strawberries, pomegranates, and in the winter, peas. I went to Porterville Junior College for a semester, then decided to go to Cal State because there was little work for me, and I didn't want to be a burden on Tom. After graduating from Cal I went to UCSF for pharmacy school, where I graduated with honors and second in the class. While at UCSF, I met a lab tech named Ellen Shimada during lunch in the hospital cafeteria. I asked several gals to be my date for the UCSF student dances, and they all said they'd let me know and never would. I asked Ellen for the first time, and she said yes without hesitation. After, I asked her to be my date for all the dances. The semester I met her, I fell in love and got my first C in pharmacy school because I spent all my time with her.

Hayward, California

Since I went to college on the GI Bill, I was obligated to serve in the Korean War. After, I settled down in Hayward, California, in the only neigh-borhood we could find that would sell homes to Japanese Americans.

Independent pharmacies wouldn't hire Asian Americans (or women), so I found a job at Walgreens and was grateful. Later I opened my own drugstore, Palmwood Pharmacy in San Leandro, with my wife Ellen. We had three kids—Dale, Gary, and Lois—then, later, four grandkids. I worked as a retail pharmacist until I was eighty-nine. Now, I'm ninety-five, retired, and still at my home in Hayward, California.

FRED SHIMASAKI

Joe Uzuru Shimasaki

I was delivered by Dr. Fillmore on the thirtieth of April, 1932, a half mile south of Sunnyside School in Strathmore, California, during the Depression. My sister Rinko says she was at home when I was born. Father named me after seeing a Japanese movie. There was a boy, named Yuzuru, who was a nice boy, so Father named me after him. On my birth certificate my name was written "Uzuru"—however, years later I had my name officially changed to Joe Uzuru Shimasaki.

I guess everyone remembers December 7, 1941. We were playing in the yard at Japanese School. Mr. Sekiguchi, our schoolteacher, told us Pearl Harbor was bombed by the Japanese, and we were sent home. Some weeks later, my sister Atsuko, the smart Shimasaki of the family, said because of the number of boys in the family, it was quite likely that one would be killed in the war. Also, she said that in World War I the Germans in this country were treated quite badly. She didn't think that would happen to people of Japanese ancestry. People are so much better now—not so nasty.

The war progressed, and things went from bad to worse. Restrictions were made and a curfew imposed. My brother Walt couldn't go to a school class picnic at Mooney Grove Park in Visalia, because it was too far from home. There was a question of whether the people on the east side of Highway 65 could go to Strathmore High School, which was on the other side of the road.

Eventually, we had to register for the evacuation. It seems like we spent all day in line. Some weeks later, it came time to take a bus to Fresno Assembly Center with one suitcase of clothes. The day before I left for camp, I told my teacher I would not be in school anymore because I had to go to camp. She said she was sorry to see this happen. The day we went to camp we drove by the Sunnyside School. I could see the kids playing in the yard. I knew this would not be a part of my life anymore. I also hid myself so they could not see me.

Fresno Assembly Center

In the spring of 1942, I was just ten years old when I went to the Fresno Assembly Center. We had more lines—chow lines; we wore the number 13850 pinned to our clothes; suitcases inspected for contraband. We had a series of three typhoid shots. The first made you sick and your arm sore for a week; the rest just made your arm sore. When I go to the Fresno Fair and see the ponies run, I can

Joe Shimasaki.

just about tell where I used to live. The place seems a lot smaller now. The barracks were tar-papered without any gypsum board or drywall. The floors had space between them and alfalfa growing through the cracks. . We all lived in one room. A sheet was hung on a wire to create some privacy. One time, I had to make a mad dash while I was stark naked to get behind the sheet. Ruth Hirose, Rink's friend, saw me. We slept on army cots with straw-filled mattresses. There were separate buildings for the showers and toilets. The toilets had two rows of toilet holes over a galvanized trough. It also had a tank on one end that had a constant flow of water. When the tank became full, it would trip and wash the waste away, right itself again, and fill with water again. If you weren't careful, you could get splashed.

Jerome Relocation Center

In the fall of 1942, we were transferred to Denson, Arkansas. We rode an old train that took us about four or five days to get there. The train must have been the oldest one in the country. The upholstery had a musty smell. The cars had slack between them, so when the train started up, it would jerk, and when it stopped, it was like an accordion. All was not bad on the train. You couldn't sleep well, but the food was great. There was a diner with Negro waiters. For breakfast they served us pork sausage with tender scrambled eggs. It was the first time I ate pork sausage—the eggs I used to cook were always like rubber. In Arkansas it was mud to your ankles and diarrhea. Denson was muddy when we got there, and everyone got diarrhea. It didn't make any difference what water you drank. It was the type of diarrhea that when you had to go, you had to go right then! After several weeks, everyone got well. There were scraps of lumber around left over from the construction of the camp, and people would make furniture for themselves. We were given gypsum board to make the room more livable. We were also given more room. We had regular toilets and mattresses. The men would chop trees and saw wood for the stoves. Things were still in a mess when we got there. School didn't start until several months after September. We kids had a lot of time to fool around. Once, we went to see what the "outside" was like. The Army guard would walk in one direction to a certain point, turn around and walk in the other direction. When he turned around, we crawled through the barbed-wire fence, dashed across the road, and jumped into a ditch on the other side. Months later, the guards were gone, and we would climb up the guard towers to look around.

Life in Jerome Relocation Center, Denson, Arkansas

We spent over two and a half years in Arkansas—part in Jerome Relocation Center at Denson, then later in Rohwer Relocation Center at McGehee. When we first got to Jerome, there were a lot of Negro workers working on the camp. We were not accustomed to seeing Black people. It worked both ways—neither were they used to seeing people like us. Once we saw this fellow doing a kind of dance like tap dancing. I was really impressed. Another time we watched them playing craps. They kept up a chatter—like, "Baby needs shoes," etc.—when they threw the dice. It was very interesting. We kids used to try to hunt rabbits with clubs, but the Negroes were much better. They would form a large circle around a field and tighten the circle. The rabbits were clubbed when the ring of men was small, and the rabbits didn't have anywhere to go.

We used to have things like mud fights. Once I put a bunch of grass on a mud ball and threw it at a bigger guy. He saw me, chased, and pelted me with a handful of mud balls at close range. I learned something that day—NEVER ATTRACT ATTENTION! We would also make up football teams and challenge other teams from different blocks. We would practice plays and play tackle football without pads or helmets. It was a rough game.

During the early part in Arkansas, there was a young gang leader named Rabbit. He must have been about sixteen—a local terror. When the odds were right, he and his cohorts would pick on someone. But, if Rabbit was caught in other circumstances, he would run like a rabbit. That's how he got his name. One evening a bunch of judo experts decided to straighten Rabbit out. There were hundreds of onlookers there, including myself. Not much happened—maybe a minor scuffle. But after that, we didn't hear about Rabbit anymore.

The Sears, Roebuck catalog was our department store, and *Life* magazine was our news source. Once there were pictures in *Life* of typical meals that a GI ate during a week. It may have been made to look better than it was, but it sure did look good to me. Paul Strate visited my brother Fred in camp for two or three days on his way to the war in Europe. This was a bit unusual, but he said they didn't give him any trouble at the gate or Administrative Building. He must have had a hard time, because we were having a run on fish at the mess hall. Just about every meal, except breakfast, was fish. The fish wasn't too bad, and I liked the squid. The salt pork and rice weren't too bad, but I don't think I would ever go to a store and buy salt pork to take home to eat—not now.

On occasion we used to go fishing outside of camp. The first time I used a bent straight pin for a hook, a string, and a limb for a pole. Later, we used regular hooks. We used to drag a piece of pork on a string, and crawdads would grab hold of it. We would use them for bait. There was an old man, named Kishi, who used to take us fishing. His son was in the air force, which was unusual at that time. He was proud of his son and would show us pictures of him.

During one period, everyone started to make rings. Some people would get a quarter, slowly tap the edges with a hammer to form a silver band, and cut the center out. Others would get a nut off a bolt and slowly file until they formed a ring. To make a long story short, a few of us kids were turned in for stealing nuts. The older kids would tell me I was going to jail. I told them that I was in the can already. They would tease me about the jail with steel bars at Monroe. I had to go with the block manager to see someone at the Administrative Building. We waited a long time, saw someone about a couple of minutes, and that was the end of it.

During a homeroom class, some of the students asked a young twenty-five-year-old Caucasian teacher, "How come we're in camp?" It was one of the few times we talked about it to a teacher. We had a good frank discussion. She mentioned she had a husband in the service in Italy, and if she didn't think she was doing good by teaching us, she would quit. She asked what those paper fish were doing hanging on the poles. She said, "You should become more American." When I see those paper fish, I think—become more American—and I remember her.

Mom (Hatsu Shimasaki) used to make me go to Sunday school. At Christmas the churches in the Midwest would send Christmas presents to the children in camp. I can remember receiving such things as jigsaw puzzles and pick-up sticks. I can remember two occasions when we made ice cream in camp. One time was when George Enosaki was there visiting. We scrounged around the mess hall for canned milk, eggs, and whatever we needed. Then we took the stuff out to the hospital. We made it in a huge garbage can filled with ice. A large milk can was stuck inside the container for the ice cream.

Shimasaki brothers, Joe and Walt.

Rohwer Relocation Center

When Mother became ill, my brother Walt and I were the only ones still in camp. We used to sweep and mop the floors every day and go to the washroom, where we hand-washed our clothes with a bar of soap and washboard. There were no washing machines in camp. Our cousins notified Rink that Mother was ill, and she should come home immediately.

Tooele, Utah, 1945

Later, we made a trip to Utah where our eldest brother Tom was at Tooele. Our mother had a hard time on that trip. Later, the doctors said to let her have anything she wanted. She wanted watermelon once, so I went to the grocery store to get some. Walt got a job as a dishwasher, and Mama got really upset. She made him quit that job.

Mother passed away. Rink said Mother wanted her family money to go to the three youngest kids. It amounted to around $165 to $225 each. Tom drove his wife Mitsuye, son Bob, daughter Janet, Walt, and myself back to Lindsay straight without sleep from Utah.

Seven years later, Fred was out of pharmacy school, Walt was in dental school at UCSF Medical Center, and I was at UC Berkeley in pre-pharmacy—with flea bites all over my body from picking tomatoes at the Sonodas in Oceanside. Eventually, Walt moved to Eureka, California, married Jean, raised three boys (Mike, Paul, and Allen), and retired after decades working as an oral surgeon. I moved back to live in Visalia, where I married Rosalie, and retired after a long career as a pharmacist. Rosalie and I avidly skied every winter. We've taken thirty-eight trips overseas, traveling the world together from the Galápagos Islands to Mongolia to Egypt to New Zealand, and we're still traveling today!

Tim Taira

Relocation Recollections

I was nine years old when I was interned and twelve when I was released. I was first sent to the Fresno Assembly Center in Fresno, California, then moved to Jerome, Arkansas, and finally Rohwer, Arkansas. Prior to internment in 1942, I was in the third grade. I watched my parents struggle with preparations for three days and nights. We were ordered out of our home on departure day, when I also bade my pet dog Romper farewell.

Fresno Assembly Center

This was our first stop, a hastily constructed camp at the Fresno County Fairgrounds. The Assembly Center was designed like a prison. The barracks were enclosed behind barbed-wire fencing, with guard towers and armed sentries patrolling the perimeter on foot. The barracks themselves were bare except for army cots; weeds were growing through the wide cracks in the floor. The interior spaces were not partitioned for families, who used canvas or bedsheets for privacy. We were provided with mattress covers and ordered to fill them with hay. The hay was infested with fleas and other bugs and everyone was bitten. The most miserable part was the heat. There was no provision for cooling during the hot (over 105°F) Fresno summer. Electric fans were specifically prohibited as contraband. Facilities were all communal. School was conducted in horse barns with only an open door to provide light and ventilation. The volunteer teachers stood the whole time, while the students sat on bales of hay. We had centralized dining, latrines, washrooms, all unpartitioned. There were long lines for our unappetizing meals. Without refrigeration, our food quickly spoiled in the summer heat. An entire block of over two hundred was stricken by food poisoning, with no medical help available. The entire medical supply for the emergency was castor oil and alcohol. The restrooms overflowed with everyone in need of relief. The limited facilities could not accommodate so many—it was a very messy scene.

The center's hospital was another single-story barracks-type building with rows of cots. Expectant mothers received a special ration of one orange per day. A teenager was assigned the duty of distributing the oranges throughout the center, and I volunteered to help him in anticipation of my own orange if any were left over.

There was much gossip about our future "permanent" home in Arkansas. An unknown area, remote and wild; alligators and snakes were feared.

The Move to Arkansas

Dad volunteered us for the first group, called the Advance Crew. Its task was to get the camp ready for others and to report back on the conditions in Arkansas. When the move came, we were herded into old rickety train cars. Mom expressed sorrow as we saw our house slowly disappear. As we left Fresno, the shutters were ordered closed for the entire trip. The first stop to stretch our legs occurred somewhere in the desert. Internees piled out on one side facing a row of soldiers, who had their guns pointed toward us somewhat in the manner of a firing squad. My kid brother was four months old and on formula, so Mom started walking toward the locomotive to find hot water for rinsing his dirty bottles. One soldier raised his rifle and threatened to shoot if she didn't stop. She explained her purpose and kept walking, and the soldier decided not to shoot. That's what mothers did for their babies back then. Back on the train, the conductor grabbed two dirty bottles from Mom's hands and said he would rinse them. He was gone so long that I thought the conductor might have stolen the bottles and said as much to Mom, but she reassured me otherwise. Later he returned the bottles, which had been sterilized. He repeated this during the rest of the trip, and I've never forgotten this act of basic kindness.

Jerome

When we finally reached our "permanent" home, we found a similar setup to the Fresno Assembly Center, except larger, more spacious,

and better con-
structed. Although
the camp was not
yet finished, camp
security in the usual
form of barbed-wire
fencing and guard
towers with search-
lights was in place.
Construction and
ditching operations
were still in progress;
the plumbers gam-
bled all day with dice
while the camp kids did much of the actual work, mainly threading pipe,
for ten cents an hour. The barracks were on open ground, with forests
and swamps beyond.

Larry, Gene, and Tim Taira.

We had exchanged the dry desert heat of Fresno for Arkansas humidity. In Jerome it was muggy in the summer and icy in the winter. I encountered sleet for the first time in my life and enjoyed eating the icicles that
hung from the eaves. The soil of Jerome was clay, which became sticky
and slippery when wet. You got taller with every step.

We entered the food chain of the abundant local insect life. I particularly recall the annoying chiggers, which targeted the most tender and
sensitive parts of your body. I also encountered fireflies for the first time.
We caught them in jars, but they soon quit glowing in captivity. There were
many, many spiders preying on the other insects, and I entertained myself
watching the chain of events when bugs became ensnared in their webs.

Reptiles were varied and numerous. I saw all four of the American
venomous snakes here and was particularly warned to avoid coral snakes.
Once bitten by one of these, you were as good as dead—there was no
antivenin available. I took this warning seriously! The older kids used to
scare us with tales of the blue racer, a snake so fast you couldn't outrun it.
Worse yet was the brown hoop snake, which curled into a hoop and came
rolling after you. I was suckered by these stories for a long time, and even
carried a stick to beat them off if they ever attacked me. I felt quite foolish
later. The only confirmed venomous bite I know of was delivered by a pet
rattlesnake. Its owner had filed down its fangs and didn't realize that they
would grow back. I foolishly asked Mom for permission to keep a pet

rattlesnake of my own. Her response was predictably harsh and negative. I secretly proceeded with my plan, which ultimately failed because I could not find a suitable hiding place to keep it.

There were plenty of lizards, turtles, and tortoises around and I even encountered a mossback turtle. There were no alligators then, but I understand there are some living there now, having invaded some fifteen years ago.

I was most fond of the fascinating variety of fish and other aquatic life. Strange fish like the drum, buffalo fish, and gar intrigued me. There were others that I never identified: I recall spotting a strange white, snakelike creature with gills and tiny legs near its head, but I was unable to capture a specimen for identification. I used to poke my hand into crawfish holes and pull them out. They were large and strong enough to break my skin with their pincers, but I got them out. One day I encountered a hole that was larger and drier than usual, so I took the precaution of poking inside with a stick before using my hand. Out popped a snake—a close call!

Dad was a camp doctor and practically lived at the hospital to handle emergencies. Mom was tied down with an infant, and I was left unsupervised. I took full advantage of the situation and was soon totally out of control. I learned how to sneak out of camp and explore the surrounding forest and swamp. Once when I was exploring the forest, I spotted a round, ball-like object on the ground and decided to kick it and watch it roll. Immediately a swarm of angry hornets flew out and began stinging me repeatedly. I ran faster and faster, but not nearly fast enough. On another occasion I chased a rabbit into the forest and suddenly realized I had completely lost my bearings. No one knew where I was and I dreaded the consequences of discovery, so I decided to walk in an outward spiral in hopes of finding a familiar landmark. It eventually worked, and I was able to keep the incident secret until recently.

I collected cigarette butts and carefully salvaged the tobacco. Then I made a pipe from a long, tubular weed that had a ball at one end that I hollowed out. Whenever a doctor asks whether I've smoked and when I quit, I respond that I gave up tobacco at age eleven. The shocked looks get worse when I say that I started smoking at age nine.

Old Japanese men love soaking in hot water after bathing. At Jerome they constructed a large wooden tub and took pains to get the water in it good and hot. On hot summer days we'd risk their wrath by filling it with cool water for our own comfort. Once we were caught in the act and got chased by an old man swinging an axe. Happily for us, we could run much faster! I enjoyed "fishing" for rats under the barracks. I'd fashioned a hook from a sewing needle and threw the baited line into the cavity under the barracks. When the line moved, I yanked hard to try snagging the rat. The sport was unproductive, but great fun. My

Grandparents, Tomotaka and Momoko Taira.

grandpa had a small fishpond stocked with minnows, which I'd steal for bait. He was puzzled at the disappearances and presumed the lost minnows had been washed away in the rain. I never told him otherwise.

I was easily the worst student in our school. My grades were rock bottom and could not get any lower. I found book learning to be a bore and was much more interested in nature. I had probably learned more about the local environment than the entire class put together, including the teacher. I remember getting a message that Dad wanted to see me, which was always a bad omen. I didn't think he'd ever finish chewing me out about my low grades. I slowly improved just enough to pass, unless my teachers just wanted to be rid of me.

The adults set priorities and made numerous sacrifices in the camps to ensure that the next generation had every advantage possible under the circumstances. Their motto was *kodomo no tameni*—for the sake of the children. Instead of simply giving in to despair, they worked hard to make a tight-knit, smoothly running society. It was a working model of what they'd had prior to the camp, which was amazing given that the inmates came from widely different areas. Education, public health, fire, and police were primarily staffed and run by the inmates. The dining and recreational facilities were self-governed and supplemented with fresh produce, poultry, and pork grown by the many good farmers in the camp. There were paid jobs, but camp pay was never more than a stipend. As camp physician, Dad was the highest-paid worker in camp at $19/month (seventy to eighty hours per week); this was roughly the same as a private in the US Army. Salaries scaled down from there, and many chose to simply work without pay at whatever task needed doing.

American patriotism rarely wavered in the camps. How could a nine-year-old like me contribute? We didn't have money for war bonds, so I decided to purchase savings stamps. I carefully saved my pennies and bought stamps, which I glued into a booklet. Just before war's end, I had finally filled the entire book and hurried to the post office to trade it for a war bond. It made me so happy and proud that I never redeemed it—I still have it to this day.

Many inmates volunteered to serve in the US military, most notably in the 442nd Regimental Combat Team in Europe and in the Military Intelligence Service in the Pacific Theater. An exceptionally high proportion of those volunteers never returned. I had an uncle, Harry Kuroiwa, who served in the 442nd. His experiences were unusual in that he was one of the very few in that unit to be captured by the Germans. During a night action and in the midst of a storm, he volunteered to help his wounded platoon leader to find aid. They eventually located an aid station and rushed in, only to discover it belonged to the Germans. As a POW, the Germans found Uncle Harry fascinating, and interrogated him constantly over a period of days.

An occurrence at Jerome that remained a mystery to me for decades was the day we were inundated with Hawaiian soldiers. They handed out cookies and candy to the kids, which made us feel like we'd gone to heaven after months without sweets. Then they left as suddenly as they appeared. I only recently learned that these Hawaiians were from the 100th Battalion, which had been training at Camp Shelby, Mississippi, as part of the 442nd. The Nisei from Hawaii had not been interned and were a happy-go-lucky and gregarious bunch, quite different temperamentally from the mainland Nisei. These differences were causing considerable friction during training, so their CO had an idea. He sent busloads of the Hawaiians to Jerome, which was the closest relocation center. En route to Jerome the group was cheerful and boisterous; during the return trip there was stunned silence. They were shocked to see the families of fellow trainees imprisoned behind barbed wire. They understood the situation now, and the friction between the two Nisei groups stopped. Future senator Dan Inouye was in this group and later recounted the experience.

I recall one special act of kindness during my time in Jerome. One Christmas, a kind and generous lady in Little Rock provided a Christmas gift for every school student in the camp (even its worst!). I am unable to recall her name or why she did this, but it made a lasting impression.

Rohwer

In mid-1944 the War Department decided to convert Jerome into a POW camp. During that summer many of the former Jerome internees were sent to the camp at Rohwer, located just twenty-five miles away. The camp was not very different from Jerome, though I remember we burned wood for heat at Jerome and coal at Rohwer. Inmates here were from different areas of the country. By now the security arrangements had become relaxed; the barbed-wire fences were knocked down and the guard towers went unmanned. It proved that those stringent security measures were unnecessary in the first place. For me, this meant I could more freely and frequently visit my wilderness playground. We had a serious scare when we learned that the Mississippi River had overflowed its banks. Fortunately, the flooding didn't reach Rohwer and we didn't need to be re-relocated.

Post-Rohwer

After leaving Rohwer, we returned to Fresno, California. We Japanese were not welcome back. Some businesses and homes were vandalized, most were taunted with racial slurs, some rural properties were targeted with drive-by shootings, and we were often refused admittance to businesses. Dad reestablished his medical practice. No dealer would sell him a car that he needed to make house calls, so he made do by borrowing one from a family friend until a concerned patient finally acquired one for him.

Certain neighborhoods prohibited Japanese and other minorities from residing. Our real estate agent canvassed the neighbors before allowing our family to move into Fresno's Armenian Town. I had not a single friend and was fearful on the first day in junior high school. Rumor was that students elsewhere were stoned and beaten, but surprisingly I was personally greeted by Mr. Gillis, the school principal, who assigned two boys to look after me. These boys, Larry Avakian and Richard Mahakian, turned out to be the most respected student leaders, so they ensured that I experienced no problems. Eventually Richard and I became good friends, and we often played sports together after school and on weekends.

I served in the US Army during the period of the Korean conflict. I was sent first to a Japanese language school, then to a Korean language school. Once actually in Korea, I served with military intelligence from 1955–56. After my discharge from the Army, I attended university and received a degree in civil engineering. Both of my younger siblings also went to college; later, one went into business and the other into law enforcement. We have two children; my son Mark is an MD and my daughter Sunya is in dentistry. Our five grandchildren are either in college or working for a living. After a career in traffic engineering, I took early retirement and pursued my numerous other interests. My wife, June, and I have traveled extensively. I have also been actively researching and collecting artifacts from the Japanese wartime relocation. A friend has helped me to create a digital museum of my collection that continues to grow with the years.

May Ichinaga Takeda

December 7, 1941: World War II

Japan carried out an air strike on Pearl Harbor, Hawaii. The United States had most of its naval fleet in Pearl Harbor, when all hell broke loose!!! This affected all of us who were of Japanese descent, which included the first, second, and third generations in the United States. December 7 was on a Sunday. The next day, all my siblings went to school. They were met by many questions that they had no answers for. At the time, my father and family had a Chinese restaurant, Jim's Chop Suey. Our business had dropped overnight. That same week, there was an "order" issued, that anyone of Japanese descent would be under curfew from 6:00 p.m. till 6:00 a.m. I am sure this order came from the governor of California. However, since my dad knew the mayor and some other Tulare businessmen, they told us we could stay open until 12:00 a.m. Our customers thought we were Chinese.

Things started happening very fast! We were hearing "talks" about moving all people of Japanese descent from the coasts of California, Oregon, and Washington. In January 1942 the US government sent out an executive order to move all Japanese from the states of California, Oregon, and Washington to assembly centers first, then to move all of us farther inland, to the internment camps. Starting in January 1942, those of Japanese descent that lived along the coast were the first ones to be moved into the assembly centers away from the coast. The demarcation line was

Reprinted with permission from May Takeda et al., *All We Could Carry: James K. & Kiyono Ichinaga's Children Remember the War Years (1941–46)* (self-pub., Pleasanton, CA: 2004)

Highway 99 in California. They moved anyone living west of Highway 99 into the assembly center early in early April. Anyone living east of 99 soon followed and was moved to the assembly centers during the first week of May.

May Ichinaga Takeda, 1944.

The government had ordered us to sell, give away, or leave our property. This included homes, farms, businesses, cars, etc. This was such a hectic time for everyone. Everyone had to figure out what they could sell or must be sold. This part was easy to figure out . . . EVERYTHING! No one wanted to buy anything, so most of the families left their possessions with neighbors and friends or just gave them away. The banks took possession of much of the land. At the time, no one knew when, or if ever, we could come back to California. Father (James K. Ichinaga) was the spokesperson for the people of Japanese descent who lived in Tulare County. He had a list of what we could take and could not take. They only allowed us to take what we could individually carry . . . no extra packages!! It was especially sad saying goodbye to our friends and neighbors. On the morning of May 5, 1942, our family boarded the bus with the others of Japanese descent (from Tulare County), and left our home in Tulare, California. They transported us to the Fresno Assembly Center, which was located on the Fresno County Fairgrounds, at Kings Canyon and Maple Avenue.

May 1942–October 1942: Fresno Assembly Center

Moving into the Fresno Assembly Center was a huge ordeal. Everyone had to wait in line to be checked in by the army personnel. They checked us in, family by family, with all our packages and belongings. We then had to wait until we were assigned to our block, barrack, and rooms. After being checked in, we had to walk, still carrying what we could, to our block. They assigned us to Block D. Each block consisted of approximately sixteen barracks that housed around four hundred–plus people. Each block had a kitchen and dining area. There was one shed for the laundry, another shed for the latrine, and a shed for the showers. As you can imagine, everyone had to stand in line and wait their turn for everything. And there was No Privacy! The barracks consisted of a tar-papered frame and a rough cement floor. The dividers for the rooms were walls, from the floor to four to six inches above the door frame. Everything above that was open.

There was a single 60-watt light bulb hanging in the middle of each room. There were no other electrical outlets, no plumbing, no basins, no mirrors, tables, or chairs . . . in other words, just a bare room!! We were issued cots and straw mattresses to sleep on. That was it!! We lived out of suitcases because there were no closets, hooks, or any other means to hang our clothes. Can you imagine, leaving a comfortable home for this?

When the meals were ready to be served, the kitchen helpers would come out and bang on the tin dishpan. Everyone would have to stand in line and wait. The meals were served army mess style. No one was allowed to eat in another "block." I worked at the canteen, which was about four blocks away, and had to walk back to my own block to eat lunch and then walk back to work again.

The laundry room was used for washing clothes, getting our drinking water, ironing, and bathing the children. There were no washing machines or dryers here!

The men and women's latrines were divided by a wall with six toilet holes (the sitting bench type) on each side. There was a galvanized trough that carried the waste away (the trough was shared.) Every minute or so, the water would surge down like a tidal wave to carry the waste away. We would have to stand up, otherwise we would get splashed with . . . well, you get the picture. Some wise guy took the knots out of the planks that separated the men's and the women's sides. So, we always made it a routine to check to see that all the holes were covered before using the facility. There were no dividers between the toilet holes, again . . . No Privacy!

The showers had three shower heads on each side. Imagine, only two to three shower heads on each side, for the entire block for four hundred people!! Of course, there were always many who were waiting in lines for these showers. The men's and women's showers shared a common wall dividing them. There were no doors at the entrance, and there were no shower stalls, again . . . No Privacy!

Curfew, all lights out by 10:00 p.m. . . . . There were so many rules to follow. Every room was searched by the army officials for contraband:

scissors, knives, anything electrical, and money. This occurred the first time in June 1942 and the second time in August 1942. There were some things stolen by the army men, but not one of us uttered a peep, not knowing what the consequences would or could be.

Jobs. Just about every person eighteen years of age and older worked somewhere in camp. I worked at the canteen. We sold aspirin, toothpaste, brushes, soaps, creams, lotions, ice cream, etc. I vowed that I would never work at the canteen when we moved inland to another camp. We were so busy at the canteen; we were on our feet running and waiting on people all day. I never worked harder in my whole life!

The weather was HOT . . . HOT . . . HOT. We spent the summer in hot weather at the Fresno Assembly Center. No trees for shade, no fans or air conditioners, not even a swamp cooler! Remember, no outlets for anything electrical. Our main priority was to keep COOL!! It was quite a sight to see us with wet cloths over our heads and faces, fanning ourselves like crazy with homemade paper fans (folded like accordions). We utilized the shade of our barracks. It is a wonder we did not die of heat exhaustion!

In September 1942 a group of men from the Fresno Assembly Center traveled to Arkansas to check out the facilities. The contractors were amazed to see the Japanese men, who were as tall as themselves, who could speak English fluently. The builders had to adjust many things, because they built everything for midgets! They built the barracks to the same size specifications as the government wanted it to be built. Still, the other things like the benches and tables were built lower than average. The shower heads had to be raised. I guess they were expecting to see these Japanese people, whom they often characterized as short, skinny, with slanted eyes and wearing coolie hats! The families assigned to relocate to Jerome were the last group to leave the Fresno Assembly Center.

Journey to Internment (Concentration) Camp
Jerome, Arkansas, October 1942

They ordered the people in the Fresno Assembly Center to move inland. The internment camps were in the states of Idaho, Utah, Wyoming, Arizona, Colorado, New Mexico, and Arkansas. Starting as early as September 1942, those who wanted to join relatives in other internment camps, in other states, could do so. Those of us that went to Jerome were the last ones to leave the Fresno Center. There were two internment camps in the state of Arkansas, Rohwer and Jerome. Rohwer internment camp was close to Pine Bluff, Arkansas. The Jerome internment camp was located toward the southern end of Arkansas, close to McGehee, Arkansas.

It was towards the end of October, when we started our journey to the Jerome internment camp. This time an old, dilapidated train transported us. It took us four days to get there. Every seat was filled. There were two armed guards in each car. The guards would order us to close the canvas curtains before entering any small burg, town, or city. They would allow us to roll up the curtains again, only when the guards told us when it was okay. They locked the door to the toilet always when we traveled through the towns and cities. There was a good reason for this. The toilet had a seat, but there was no bottom, so the waste, the toilet paper, etc. was dropped straight down to be scattered in between the train tracks. I think we stopped twice on our trip to Jerome. The first time was in the desert of Arizona and the second time was in a desert in Texas. We were able to get off the train, allowed to exercise and stretch our bodies, and visit with relatives and friends in the other cars.

From the state of California, we traveled through the states of Arizona and New Mexico to Texas, down to Corpus Christi, Texas, and up to Texarkana (a border town that touches three states) . . . and then down to the Jerome internment camp. There were no hot meals on the train. We were given sandwiches and fruit in a paper bag for our meals, and there was no water to wash ourselves. We arrived at our destination in the evening and were hauled by cattle trucks to our blocks. We were so tired, hungry, and dirty. To this day, I do not know how we survived the trip! When reaching our room, I wasn't shocked to find (again) an empty room with only one 60-watt bulb hanging from the ceiling. Nevertheless, it was still nicer than the barracks in Fresno. These barracks had walls which divided the rooms, and these walls went up to the ceiling. As it turned out, our block was not yet completed, so we were invited by another block, allowing us to use their facilities, which were about one-half mile away (approximately four blocks). My friends and I endured the long walk just to take a shower that night. We shared their facilities for a couple of days.

Jerome Internment Camp: November 1942–May 1943

Again, a high, electrically wired fence surrounded our camp, with tall sentry towers built on each corner. Before we left the Fresno Assembly Center, they already assigned us the block, barrack, and rooms that we were to live in while interned in Jerome.

Most of the people eighteen years and older worked at something. There were many teachers (the children had to keep up with their studies). Nurses and doctors worked unrealistic hours for only $12 and $19 per month. They paid the rest of us $12 a month. They paid teachers only $12 per month. The camp maintained a fire department, manned by young men. This was the only emergency vehicle in camp, which also served as an ambulance. I cannot figure out how these people got the messages because there were no telephones!

The barrack rooms had wooden floors, so it was much nicer than Fresno's. There was a gully in front of the doors, and wooden slat walkways leading to a common dirt pathway. Barrack front doors faced each other. Like the doors in the Fresno Assembly Center barracks, there were no locks or keys to secure our rooms.

In camp, as well as the assembly center, there were no pets allowed, no dogs, cats, not even goldfishes. No drinking hard liquor. There were very few men who smoked. People could not afford luxury items. What could a person buy for $9 a month? No individual parties . . . no celebration of any kind unless it involved every person in the "Block." The children were also affected: no bikes, wagons, skates (or anything with wheels). There were no toys for them to play with. They played jump rope, jacks, and other childhood games like hopscotch, Simon Says, etc. Everyone had to rely on each other for entertainment. The young adults had song fests and baseball tournaments, etc. Of special interest, to me, was catching fireflies when it got dark. Since we lived in the last block in camp, there was a green, grassy area between our block and the hospital. People of all ages came to catch the fireflies. They would glow off and on. A dozen fireflies would shed enough light to see the ground. The older adults learned how to play bridge and other card games. They read the Bible and books of all kinds. There were different classes on how to sew, make paper flowers, paint, how to carve wood, etc. This was our entertainment. We were living among our friends here and made some lasting friendships in camp.

The government okayed and started a program of scattering the people of Japanese descent to different states that were willing to hire them. No one could go back to California, Oregon, or Washington or was allowed to work in any state that had the internment camps. This program was called "Indefinite Leave." We again had to be cleared by the FBI before leaving camp. No one could work in a defense factory or anything that pertained to defense. Starting in February 1943, the first group allowed to leave was the students who wanted to enter college.

The United States is my country. I will always cherish the freedom we have. GOD BLESS AMERICA.

May Ichinaga Takeda, 2003.
Photo by Norman Yamauchi.

George Teraoka

Executive Order 9066

May 13, 1942, will be well remembered. It was my twenty-first birthday that our family reported to the Fresno County Fairgrounds, designated as the Fresno Assembly Center, in compliance with President Roosevelt's Executive Order 9066. Since we were living on the west side of Highway 99, the dividing line in Central California, we were amongst the first of our area to be removed from our homes. It was the beginning of a new era in our destiny of life.

Fresno Assembly Center

Life in the assembly center, for most of us, created new challenges, and we sought ways to meet them. As for myself, there was one burning question that seemed to be uppermost in my mind, and that was what led to our incarceration without being guilty of any violation of public law. I frequently engaged in conversation with people that I had great respect for, and no one could give me a satisfying answer. Most shrugged their shoulders. Issei people usually commented with *shikata ga nai*; that literally means there is no other way. It's an expression of resignation and to comply.

Life in Fresno Assembly Center, despite being confined, became the challenge of finding peace and enjoyment of life. Looking for entertainment seemed like the only way to pass the time and still make life enjoyable. Many sought ways to make life meaningful. Along this line of thinking, I had a friend send me my small PA system with a record player to play dance music. Through this use of the equipment, I was frequently invited to small parties to play music. Most of us from Fresno Assembly

Center were transferred to the Jerome, Arkansas, camp. When the Fresno Assembly Center was to close, I volunteered to be among the last to go to help be part of the cleanup crew. My family went ahead with the rest of the contingent. After our assignments were completed, we closed the Fresno Center to board the train. It was to be my first time ever to ride a train. We were ordered to keep our window shades down, but occasionally sneaked a peek, curious as to where we were. There were no road signs along the tracks, so it was our best guess as to where we were. It was obvious when the train was slowing down that we were coming into a community. Sneaking a view of the passing communities, my lasting impression of my first train ride will always be how the trains are always on the back side of the homes, where we see junked cars and trucks rusting away, pigpens, chicken coops, horse barns, and occasionally a neatly kept garden.

Jerome Relocation Center, Arkansas

Finally, after we arrived at Jerome Relocation Center, I learned that my family address was 41-4-F and I rejoined my family. My father, Sawakaro Teraoka, was already in Jerome. I quickly found employment in the kitchen washing dishes for a month. Since my high school days, I was an FCC-licensed Amateur Radio Station professional with assigned call letters W6PUC and, being electronically minded, I opted to find employment with the Electricians group. Some of us repaired radios and other electrical equipment along with assignments related to electrical-power maintenance. Frequently, storms with lightning strikes would blow main fuses on the outdoor power lines. I had been assigned to replace the blown fuses. The scary part of the task was that the lines were drawing an arc to the fuse-replacing poles we were using, even before touching the high-tension wires. Obviously, the high-tensioned voltage was going through us to the high pole we were clamped onto. The potential difference at that point was not great enough to kill us, so it gave us a sense of confidence in the task.

From time to time the thoughts of our immediate destiny aroused thoughts of how a president through his edicts can penalize us Americans without a hearing to justify our imprisonment. Thinking back to pre-evacuation days, I was the president of our local chapter of JACL [Japanese American Citizens League], and not a peep was heard from our leadership or from our National Headquarters as to what actions to take prior to the evacuation. The sudden evacuation order made it difficult for people in business to find a successor and their businesses shut down, suffering thousands of dollars of losses, collectively running into millions. My dad, a truck farmer with forty acres, had no one interested to take over the lettuce crop harvest, suffering the loss of thousands of dollars of anticipated income. It was presumed the crop rotted in the field.

I grew up in an era where my Nisei friends were not welcomed in some of the public swimming pools in Fresno. Japanese were not the only ones discriminated against. If you were Chinese, Filipino, Mexican, or Black you were also not welcomed. We who lived in Fowler had access to Fowler High School's swimming pool in the summer, and did not experience any discrimination.

My Japanese background and customs placed me in an awkward, inferior feeling and so I wanted to be an American. I began shunning anything that was Japanese. My first thought: to be an American, I had to be Christian. A friend gave me a book to read to learn Christianity. The language that it was written in was difficult for me to comprehend. It was during this time Pearl Harbor happened. At first, we were shocked and somewhat embarrassed to hear of Japanese attacking our country. What followed was declaration of war against Japan. What prompted the president to issue Executive Order 9066, which was to clear all Japanese, US citizens or not, from the Pacific Coast, was never fully explained at the time.

What bothered me most was, why we citizens of the country would be incarcerated without a hearing to determine guilt. What was totally lacking was Nisei leadership to rebel against such obvious un-American imprisonment. There was no one among us rebelling against un-American injustice, with military herding Nisei, Sansei, as well as Issei into the relocation camps with minimal effort. As a matter of personal quest, this was the question I posed to many of my friends in camp, beginning at the Fresno Assembly Center. Of course, we were grumbling at the injustice imposed on us. When I talked to some of the Issei people I knew, the only answer that seemed to stick in my mind was *shikata ga nai*, which literally means, "there are no other ways" but to comply with the president's edict in resignation.

In the months that followed, I met many educated people who were doctors, lawyers, schoolteachers, and college professors, and posed the same question. People admitted the whole process was wrong, but could only shrug their shoulders and comply. I began to wonder what it is in the Japanese culture that allows such reasoning to tolerate injustice.

One day as I chatted with a Japanese minister, during our conversation, I commented on how we Japanese are stupid idiots. I thought we Japanese were allowing ourselves to be in camps such as this and I caught him smiling at me as I kept ranting on. When I noticed his amusement at my stupidity, I stopped. Laughingly he said, "It is obvious you don't know of the Japanese culture." I thought, what am I missing? This I've got to hear.

He first explained to me that the entire Japanese culture is based on *Muga No Kyo*. In my limited understanding of Japanese language, it meant "no self" culture or "no self" philosophy. He explained, all Japanese culture is based on this principle. This meant the asserting of the ego or self is a "No! No!" He explained that all Japanese cultural arts uphold this concept. All martial arts, kendo, judo, uphold this principle. Other arts like tea ceremony, ikebana [flower arrangement], and other cultural arts all uphold this "no self" principle. I ran into a judo instructor to have him explain to me some of their principles. When I visited their dojo, I saw people being thrown all over the place. He explained the students are learning to fall. He explained judo means "path of gentleness" when I inquired into some of their principles. He explained when in combat, let's say your opponent had a hypothetical power of 26 compared to your power of 16. It's obvious that if you asserted your power of 16, you are going to be overwhelmed by his power by 10. The whole idea is not to assert your power against him, but give your power 16 to him and maneuver yourself to take advantage of the total power of 42. In higher rank, the defendant does not assert his power of 16, but maneuvers himself in such a way as to take advantage of his power, and you are on top, selflessly rewarded.

I was fascinated, to say the least, as I began inquiring into the Japanese arts. I also observed many of my Nisei and Sansei friends were totally ignorant of our fascinating cultural heritage, and earnestly shared this understanding so we could all truly appreciate it. As the years went by, my vocal expressions of appreciation of our Japanese culture began to be heard and, before I knew it, I am now frequently asked to give talks to classes, schools, clubs, and on occasion, to be keynote speaker at conventions. To think that the beginning of my appreciation of this inspiring culture happened because of being incarcerated in Jerome, Arkansas, has made the place a sacred event in my life.

I frequently dwell on how this Japanese principle of *Muga No Kyo* has prevailed politically, socially, economically, and personally in effectively achieving desired goals. To think, everyone that was in Jerome camp was endowed with a culture that held the secret for successfully achieving a goal in life, whatever that may be. The secret was there for the seeker. Jerome has now become a sacred shrine that has guided the course of my destiny in life, a shrine to which I frequently bow spiritually in gratitude.

I was able to leave Jerome and went to St. Louis, Missouri, for the duration of the war. My family went to Rohwer Relocation Center and upon release, went home to Fowler, California. The Teraoka Farm of forty acres is still producing farm crops as of today.

This is my story. —GEORGE TERAOKA, Fowler, California

Dorothy Ichinaga Thomas

Goodbye Tulare; Hello World

Pearl Harbor—that place was the first step in my launching out into the world. This was not a voluntary step, but rather, a push from my staid world of high school into an experience which I neither understood nor appreciated.

On the Sunday night of December 7, some of the older family members were at the Jim's Chop Suey Café, cooking for customers. I was there to do dishes. Father told us to hear the news which came through the voice of Franklin Delano Roosevelt, president of the USA. He told the nation that Japan had bombed Pearl Harbor. As we huddled around the old Philco radio, fear struck my heart. I was afraid that this action by the country of my ancestors would be associated with our family. At the same time, we were taught to be loyal to our country, and I felt that I was. I was caught in the middle of a problem for which there did not seem to be a straightforward answer. We did not ask, and Father did not volunteer any opinion. He always insisted that we be loyal to the US, not even learn the Japanese language, since we were in America and had no need for it.

Very soon, curfew for the Americans of Japanese descent was published. We had to be in our homes by a certain time. What was to happen to Father's business? Father had many good friends and soon had gotten the permission to stay up until the regular quitting time, 2:00 a.m. The police car would then give him a ride home. The people of Tulare, much to their credit, did not show any signs of discrimination toward us, at least to my knowledge.

Reprinted with permission from May Takeda et al., *All We Could Carry: James K. & Kiyono Ichinaga's Children Remember the War Years (1941–46)* (self-pub., Pleasanton, CA: 2004).

The day finally came, and Mother more or less got us organized so that we older ones were responsible for two bags. Inside the suitcases and cardboard boxes were those things which families thought they needed for this indefinite stay in places they did not know about. The families were marched to the buses lined up around the old Memorial Hall. Father was going here and there as needed. It was a hot day and I felt sorry for the older folks who often just sat on the curb to wait for instruction as to where they would go.

Dorothy Ichinaga Thomas, 1948.

Father had been asked by the authorities to help organize the people who came to be put on buses. He seemed to be impressed with the trust given to him to translate, answer questions, and/or give directions. The day of departure was a confusing one but seemed to have gone without any resistance.

We met at the old Memorial Hall. There were so many people with children and suitcases and boxes wrapped with twine or rope. All were directed to a specific bus, and Dad was there for moral support. The drivers were soldiers in uniform and assisting them at the door were two soldiers with guns drawn. It was as if we were animals being herded into cattle cars for a trip to a foreboding destination. Finally, we boarded the army bus.

The feeling of being imprisoned was devastating. We found our way down the center aisle of the bus and sat in those smelly old bench seats. We were all very quiet and I tried to focus on something else but reality. There were no high school friends to wave me on to my next destination. I had previously said goodbye to a few of my classmates who seemed to be sympathetic. It was very awkward to say goodbye to teachers whom I had admired and after whom I modeled my goals and dreams for the future.

During this tense time, I had to fight back tears of great sadness as I tried to imagine life without friends who did not realize the full extent of my leaving. None of us were political and we had little thought of the various pressure groups which, little by little, forced the evacuation of innocent American citizens from the West Coast.

Shirley sat with Mother, asking pertinent questions about what was happening. She must have been about three or four. "When are we going home? I want to go home." Mother tried to shush her, and finally told her something to keep her quiet. The rest of us sat without talking the whole trip. To keep myself calm, I kept counting the rivets on the roof of the bus. How many this way and how many across. Over and over.

The temperature in the bus was hot in the afternoon sun as only it can get in the Central Valley. The percentage of Ichinagas who would get carsick, did—me included. I tried to induce sleep, but it was too hot, and my body was becoming sweaty and sticky. I just pretended to fall asleep so I wouldn't have to talk to anyone. I vowed that day I would never ride in a bus again. Goodbye Tulare.

#28408—that was the card which hung around my neck. No longer was I considered a person with a name. It seemed to be more convenient to have a number, as did many Auschwitz prisoners. One can be separated from personhood by being identified by a number, thus allowing the authorities ease in shaping and maneuvering people into groups of ten or whatever. I was depressed by the War Relocation Authority's treatment of innocent people. After being unloaded from the buses which had been our connection to our former life and home, I started hating everything.

I resented being in the Fresno Assembly Center with all those other Asian people. I resented being forced to live in the temporary quarters of the horse stalls. What would happen if the horses needed the stalls and we were still in that locality? The barracks were set up like an army post. Ten barracks facing ten others in our Block D; down the center were the mess hall, the toilets, washrooms (showers), and laundry (tubs and washboards). Nice and cozy—5,100 people would be our friends and neighbors in the center.

I resented being forced to do this and that at an appointed time which was usually announced by bugle calls over the camp loudspeaking system. Getting up to get breakfast was the pits. Someone banged away on a big pot, and people who were up and ready stood in line for their breakfast. Father was one of the head cooks in our block and later became a steward for the whole block—especially in Arkansas where he went out to negotiate for fresh fruits and vegetables.

The nursery class was held in a little "room" with dirt floors, and I was an assistant to the nursery school teacher. The children had to sit on long benches—oh well, it gave them something to do, and freed the mothers for a little while. I did not enjoy doing this job for which I was ill-equipped, and my assigned room was not any cooler than the one with the children in it. We had to watch out for melted asphalt. Such an inspiring place for children to be.

About a month after having been incarcerated, Rev. Hideo Hashimoto, a Protestant minister (now deceased, 2003), arranged to have a camp graduation ceremony. On the back of the graduation ceremony program, I see my name as one of those on the student committee for that service. I only remember that some of the high schools sent diplomas and some didn't. Tulare Union High School did not ever send me a diploma and for others like me, we went through the line with the others, receiving a rolled-up paper tied with a ribbon. (In 1992, at the fiftieth reunion of the class of 1942, I was presented a nice replica of the original diploma.)

I resented the fact that the high school, which I had respected all those years, did not have the decency to send me my diploma which I earned. Of course, I was not the only one ignored by the school districts, but I felt another arrow of discrimination.

Through all this pretend situation, I did meet a fellow through the graduation committee, and I "wore" his silver football for several weeks. When I decided that I did not really want to go steady, I gave his football back. I guess he was disappointed; but this was camp, and the regular rules were not dignified by many.

We found out that the family was not the center of our focus, and independence from mother and father was easy under those circumstances. We had the three connecting bedrooms in the barracks. I pitied the families on both ends of the barracks. Mother gave us more than one lecture on being quiet.

One of the things I remember was the day we all had to get tetanus shots since we inhabited the horse stalls. Very painful experience for most of us. Some of the guys tried to be macho, but you cannot ignore a great big red arm which throbbed with pain night and day. The guys went around punching each other on the arm. Stupid guys! Hop Uchita, one of the Tulare guys, had his shot and came over to visit, I guess. He sat at the table and passed out. Hop and his brother Soichi (Switch) lived in the country with their widowed mother and a mentally retarded young man. Father was a "surrogate" father to them, as they were included in fishing trips, etc. Nice fellows.

Denson, Arkansas? Hello World! We were told to pack up to leave California to go to a little place in Arkansas. The new friends were asking one another where they would be going. Some were going to Arkansas, too, so at least I would know somebody when we got there.

We boarded what I thought was the oldest train on the tracks. It was rickety and made all sorts of noises when it tried to get started and if it had to make a turn in the route here and there, up and down. The weather was still very hot. I do not remember much of the trip except that I made myself try to sleep so I could stand that slow train and the horrible heat.

After awakening the fourth day, I asked Mother where we were, and she said we were still in Texas. When we finally got to Denson, I was pretty sick. I saw the army barracks arrangement for us again. Strange—around each block was a very deep ditch. We were told that when the rains come, the ditch would take care of the drainage of the excess of water. What kind of primitive system was this?

In order to go to the store, or visit a friend in another block, we had to very carefully step on those bobbing planks with little pieces of wood strips to help keep us on the narrow bridge. No place for children and even we older ones were very careful of using the "bridge."

Little did we know that when the winter winds came roaring in, we would have to watch our steps as it got icy there with snow and sleet. The Arkansas clay dirt was no help under these circumstances. There were no shoes or boots to help us get around. What did we do?

Good thing the carpenters' shop had a cheerful bunch of young men there. They made *getas* (go-aheads) out of pieces of odds-and-ends lumber—usually packing boxes. The sole had one hole for material which would go between the great toe and the next toe, and two side holes, each side of the instep, for the material to go through and be knotted on the other side.

What about the clay which accumulated between the wood which kept the foot up from the mud? One had to find a stick to poke the clay away until the trip was finished. You could be walking with two huge clumps of clay under your feet if you were too lazy to poke the clay away.

The carpenters who made the *getas* were very popular and I remember one sign which said, "If you want getas, geta hell out of here." They must have whipped up those things easily—for a population of more than five thousand, that would mean ten thousand *getas*! Wow! That was a lot.

Our introduction to the facilities was pitiful, ridiculous, and yet funny. The laundry sinks were plumbed very close to the floor. Oh, my back—when washing the sheets and towels. The mess hall tables were built for little children because the builders were told that we were "little people." In order to sit at the mess hall tables, we had to approach it side-saddle, and swing our legs under the table. Everything else was the same disgusting situation. Stand in line for using the toilet—one in and one out.

The toilets were always busy. It was impossible to have privacy there. Someone put up a little yardage divider for the ladies and I appreciated it. The showers did not have curtains—just get under the water and bathe. I was not used to that and it offended me. The army personnel did not have to put up with those kinds of situations, I am sure.

Dorothy Ichinaga Thomas, 2003. *Photo by Norman Yamauchi.*

The barbed-wire fence around the camp was very much in evidence, and guard towers stood at all four corners. Men were up there with guns—not to shoot people who wanted to come (who in Arkansas would want to?), but to shoot any ambitious person who wanted to go outside the barbed-wire fence.

Father was again appointed steward and got to go "outside" to buy fresh commodities.

One day he decided to get some beer and he saw two signs outside the bar. One said, "White" and the other said, "Colored." Not knowing what to do, he decided to go in the "Colored" door. The bartender said angrily, "Go out and come in the other door." This was one of the few times I can recall when discrimination seemed to weigh in his favor. It must have disturbed the bartender since his black-and-white world was interrupted by a problem non-white, but not Black.

What did people do at the Denson relocation camp? They continued with most of the activities established at Fresno Assembly Center. The young people went to temporary barracks made into schoolrooms. In the high school annual book, there were photos and acknowledgments of the Ichinagas in school life.

Many of you will face situations of adversity in the future. I would suggest that you think about how little we could take into the internment camps, but how much we were able to take from that life-altering experience. We do not wish that you would need to go through a similar situation; but if you are faced with difficult days, try to fill them with some order, which can make life more understandable and perhaps give you intensity in your purpose.

Joanne Setsu Kitano Wong

Kitano Family

My parents, Joe and Tomoye Kitano, were married on March 2, 1941. Soon after, Joe, a pharmacist, opened a small drugstore in Visalia, California, and my parents began their life together. A door separated the drugstore from the few rooms that became the newlyweds' living quarters. While Dad was establishing his new business, Mom was busily making their new home cozy and comfortable as the young couple embarked on their American Dream. Within a year, that dream was shattered when Japan bombed Pearl Harbor and Executive Order 9066 was signed.

When they found out they were assigned to the Poston Relocation Center in Arizona, Dad requested they be allowed to go to either Tanforan, where his family was ordered to go, or to the Fresno Assembly Center where Mom's family would be. They were granted permission to live temporarily at the Fresno Assembly Center, which made sense, since their home in Visalia was less than an hour away from Fresno.

My parents began preparing for the forced move they would soon be facing. Since each person could bring only what he or she could carry, the rest of their belongings needed to be stored or gotten rid of. Dad said the lady who owned the drugstore building offered to take care of things left behind, including Mom's wedding gown, wedding gifts—many of which hadn't been used yet—and Dad's new typewriter. The store inventory needed to be sold quickly. A man offered Dad an insulting $500 for stock worth $6,000. Dad refused the offer, choosing to throw his inventory away instead.

By April 1942, Mom and Dad moved into temporary quarters at the Fresno Fairgrounds. Their new home was a horse stall. Dad signed up to work in the pharmacy. Thus, he and Mom were part of the advance crew that was sent on the first train to permanent facilities in Jerome, Arkansas. On October 6, 1942, Mom and Dad began their journey to Jerome.

Mom told me that during the train ride to Arkansas, they were instructed to draw the shades on the train windows. Periodically the train would make a stop, and the passengers were allowed to get out and stretch under the watchful eyes of military personnel pointing guns at them so they wouldn't escape. Mom thought this was ridiculous, because their stops were typically in the middle of the desert where there was no place to escape to.

A camp surrounded by barbed wire with military guards posted in watchtowers welcomed the young couple to their new home. They learned they would be living on Block 14. Their home consisted of one room in an army-style barrack with partitions not quite reaching the ceiling, separating them from their neighbors' rooms. There was very little privacy. Mom and Dad each had an army cot to sleep on. A bare light bulb provided light for them and a wood-burning stove, heat.

Comments made by both Mom and Dad were that the food was terrible, and for Mom, the rows of toilets with no partitions were quite embarrassing. She said that she would often wait until late at night to use the toilet, hoping that no one else would be there. Of course, everyone else had the same idea.

For leisure activity, Dad played on the hospital baseball team called the Goombas. Mom spent her leisure time visiting with friends. Four months after their arrival in Jerome, Mom and Dad learned that they were to have an addition to their family. Me! Mom now added knitting baby sweaters to her activities.

I, Joanne Setsu Kitano, arrived on November 2, 1943, at 5:45 a.m. Dr. Kikuo Taira, a longtime family friend of Mom's family, delivered me. He would later be our family doctor when we returned to Fresno.

With a new baby in tow, Mom was quite busy now. She told me that her mother, Grandma Tachino, lived several blocks away from us, but every day she walked the distance to wash my diapers. Although Grandma worked as a cook in the mess hall, she found time each day to help Mom out.

When Jerome was converted to a German prisoner-of-war facility, Mom, Dad, and I were moved to Rohwer on June 6, 1944. While in Rohwer, Dad was given permission to work outside the camp. He went to Cincinnati, Ohio, where he applied for two jobs. One was at a children's hospital pharmacy, the other at a factory, manufacturing rings. He was offered the factory job first and accepted it. From his experiences of rejection when applying for jobs at Caucasian-owned drugstores or hospitals in California, he thought his chances of getting a job at the pharmacy were slim. There were nine applicants for the hospital pharmacy position, and Dad was eventually selected. He was surprised and honored, but out of loyalty to the person who hired him first at the factory, he decided to make rings.

In July 1945, Mom notified Dad that they were to be released from camp and could go back to California. Dad returned to Rohwer as soon as he could.

With no home to return to, our first night was spent in the basement of the Fresno Buddhist Church. The next day, Mom's cousin, Kelly Arakawa, came to pick us up and take us to his ranch, which became housing for several relatives. When Grandma's tenants vacated her house, we lived with Grandma. After resettling in Fresno, Mom and Dad went to Visalia to claim their belongings, only to find that everything had been stolen. During that time, Dad decided that he wanted to settle in his hometown, Oakland. He applied for a job at Providence Hospital in Oakland. Upon his arrival at the hospital, he was greeted by the interviewer with, "What'd you come back to the West Coast for?" Dad explained that he had been born and raised in Oakland, but his explanation fell on deaf ears. Dad mentioned that he was applying for another job at a nearby hospital in Berkeley. The interviewer called the Berkeley hospital and told their interviewer not to hire him.

Dejected, Dad returned to Fresno where he was hired to run a small family-owned pharmaceutical lab manufacturing cough syrups and various other medications. Eventually he was hired by the county hospital in Fresno, where he worked until he retired.

Although having gone through the internment was a hardship in Mom and Dad's lives, they expressed their hopes for us and future generations in our family to never have to suffer the pain of discrimination they had endured. Dad once told his granddaughter, Julie, that the part of the internment that hurt him the most was not the loss of money or belongings, but a loss of respect for the pledge of allegiance he had grown up reciting, for the flag he saluted, and for the country that was founded on the idea of freedom and justice, yet threw its citizens into concentration camps.

Dad's feelings regarding his experience of the internment softened, however, with the passage of the Civil Liberties Act of 1988, apologizing for the government's actions and granting reparations to all those interned by the government in World War II. The letter of apology he received from President George H. W. Bush meant a lot to him. He felt that the bitter experience that the internees had to endure ultimately validated their worthiness as loyal citizens and that the United States government realized that a great injustice was done to them.

Ode to Bench 27002

Oh, Wooden Bench, rustic and worn looking,
"J.H. Kitano 27002" written on your side.
You were built by my father, Joe Kitano,
from a wooden crate,
perhaps once carrying fruit or vegetables
to Jerome, Arkansas.
What purpose did you serve?
Were you the one and only piece of furniture
owned by my parents,
Joe and Tomoye Kitano, internees #27002,
while imprisoned in an internment camp
because of their ethnicity?
Upon their release, they brought you to California
where you lived for the next 68 years
in the Kitano home.
Perhaps you reminded them of the hardships they endured,
the few possessions they owned,
and their loss of freedom
when they were abruptly sent to
a bleak and barren Jerome, Arkansas
to live for the next 3 years.
You remained a part of their lives,
until they passed on.
But you survived and returned to Arkansas

where you now reside, in the McGehee Internment Museum,
a few miles from where you came.
Visitors can see you, feel you, and reflect on
the struggles and hardships Joe and Tomoye endured
with hopes that freedom would never be taken
from anyone else again.

The card reads: "Bench was made at Jerome camp by Hiroshi
Joe Kitano. Family number 27002 is stenciled on it. Donated
by Joanne Kitano Wong, daughter of Joe. Joanne was born at
Jerome November 1943."

Sharon Osaki Wong

The Power of *Gaman*

My parents, Takaji and Oritsu Osaki, came from Hiroshima, Japan, to California around 1920. They worked for Caucasian fruit farmers in Placer County near Sacramento and had four daughters, Toshiko, Sachiko, Natsuye, and Michiko. In 1938, they bought an eighty-acre plum and pear farm.

After years of hard work, the farm finally became profitable. However, everything changed in 1942 when my family and hundreds of thousands of other Japanese living on the West Coast were forcibly removed from their homes and moved to poorly constructed buildings in remote areas. They had only days to sell whatever they could and pack a suitcase for each member of the family. They had no idea where they were going and for how long.

Arboga Assembly Center–Tule Lake Internment Center

In May 1942 my family was first sent to Arboga Assembly Center in Marysville, California. Then in June 1943 they were incarcerated at Tule Lake Relocation Center in Northern California. My father was forty-one years old, my mother thirty-nine, and my sisters were nineteen, fifteen, twelve, and six.

Jerome, Arkansas: I Was Born—Sharon Osaki

After a year at Tule Lake, they were moved to Jerome, Arkansas, where I was born in 1944. After four girls, my dad was sure I would be a boy since

I was born a day before Boys Day. He planned a big celebration at the mess hall where he worked. My oldest sister had to tell him it was daughter #5, a big disappointment, but my family did qualify for an extra room!

Gila River, Arizona

When I was a month old, the government closed the Jerome camp and our family was moved once again, this time to Gila River, Arizona, from June 1944 to May 1945.

World War II Ended

When World War II ended, all the camps were closed, and the Japanese were released. Some chose to return to Japan; however, many stayed in the US. Some returned to the West Coast, others went to the East, Midwest, or South.

Our family was fortunate to get their farm back, but many other families had nothing to return to and had to start all over. It was difficult being incarcerated but even harder to start over.

As they did during incarceration, my parents chose to practice *gaman*, a Japanese word meaning tolerance, patience, perseverance. They chose to not discuss their incarceration with their children or others. I personally never heard anything from my parents or older sisters. They felt it was better to move forward, rebuild their lives, and give their children the best education possible.

After several generations, Japanese Americans realized how important the internment story is and have been educating others at the Japanese American National Museum in Los Angeles, California, and regional museums in San Jose and at internment sites across the country. As the internees are passing away, it is critical to interview as many as possible.

I am so happy when I hear from students who are studying the internment story because I think it is especially important for young people to know what happened and to not let it ever happen again.

Since I was born in camp, I have no actual memories. However, I have become very interested since my first visit to my Arkansas birthplace in 2014. I had a chance to visit the Jerome and Rohwer camp sites and visit the Japanese American Internment Museum in McGehee, Arkansas. They hold a reunion for internees every April; my husband and I have attended four reunions since 2014. Many of the other internment sites also hold annual reunions. I have met many fellow Arkansas internees and we all enjoy getting together.

I now volunteer at the Japanese American Museum (JAM) of San Jose, where visitors learn about early immigration of Japanese to America, their leadership in the agricultural community, their incarceration during World War II, and the challenges they faced while adapting and contributing to West Coast communities. JAM San Jose does a wonderful job of educating visitors, including many school groups, as well as sending speakers to schools and other organizations.

My parents and two oldest sisters have passed away but everyone in our family will forever be thankful for their *gaman*, enduring the unbearable with patience and dignity.

Mits Yamamoto

My Years between 1942 and 1946

My incarceration started at a train station in Elk Grove, California, in May 1942, leaving for destination unknown, which turned out to be Fresno Assembly Center in Fresno, California. After a few months, we were on a train again with shades down, which made it worse; we could not see anything. After about four days we arrived at a desolate area they called Jerome, Arkansas.

Denson High School, Jerome, Arkansas

My life experience started after I was fortunate enough to be included in the first graduating class of 1943, Denson High School, Jerome, Arkansas, at the age of seventeen.

My friend (who was later my brother-in-law) was always looking for things to do, so he frequently went to the office area to look for outside seasonal employment. One day he asked me to consider going with him, to a CYO (Catholic Youth Organization) Boys Camp on the outskirts of Chicago as a kitchen helper. After getting permission from my parents, since I was only seventeen, we were on our way to Chicago Heights, Illinois. Normally, this camp was to get teenage boys from the city off the sidewalk and enjoy country life, but during wartime, they were there to help farmers harvest their crops.

After a few weeks, we had a disagreement, so we quit and left for Chicago and found work at Cuneo Press. They printed all kinds of books, dictionaries, and pamphlets. When you are on seasonal leave, you are supposed to return to camp as soon as the original employment ends, but we fudged a little and enjoyed a few extra weeks of freedom. After several weeks, the WRA (War Relocation Authority) caught up with us and sent us back to camp.

In January of 1944, my friend found another job in Sarasota, Florida, which we found later was the home base of Ringling Brothers and Barnum and Bailey Circus. There were six of us recruits from Jerome. It was on an island near Sarasota, Florida, off the Gulf of Mexico. This was a small resort-like hotel called Whispering Sands.

I thought it was great, being in a warm Florida climate, instead of miserable Arkansas weather. As I turned eighteen there, I learned how to set and wait on tables dressed in a white suit and a tie. We also dusted,

James Imahara (left, in uniform) and Mits Yamamoto, circa 1946. James was the cousin of Walter Imahara, named after Walter's father.

mopped, vacuumed, and made beds without fitted sheets. Also I cleaned toilets; what a shock to do such work, but very helpful later in life. We were the handymen, did everything to run a hotel, a far cry from a country boy who depended on his mother for every little thing. What an experience. With our spare time, which was very little, we really enjoyed the sandy beaches and the warm water, which was a few hundred yards away. In May 1944, we got a call from Jerome, "Come back, we are being transferred to Gila, Arizona." All good things must come to an end; we left shortly thereafter.

Seabrook Farms, New Jersey

After arriving in Arizona, we got itchy feet again and we decided to go to Seabrook Farms in Bridgeton, New Jersey, which, I found out later, was a part of Birds Eye Frozen Foods. There our job was to quick-freeze blueberries. In that factory, we worked side by side with German POWs.

While there, we worked twelve-hour shifts, 6 to 6, switching every two weeks. On our long weekends when we got off 6 p.m. on Friday, we did not need to go back to work until 6 p.m. on Monday. We were able to do some sightseeing. Among our choices, we visited Philadelphia to see the Liberty

Bell, and New York City to see the high-kicking Rockettes at the Radio City Music Hall. We also were able to see the Frank Sinatra show and other attractions. What an experience for an eighteen-year-old farm boy. While on the streets of the Big Apple, we strained our necks to see all the skyscrapers, like the Empire State and the Chrysler building. It was a sight to remember for someone who seldom had seen buildings much higher than a few stories.

Mits Yamamoto, Camp Reunion 2019. McGehee, Arkansas.

Since this was wartime and airplane travel was in its infant stages, all the traveling was on trains or buses, with soldiers galore. We, with enemy's faces, had many scary but memorable moments. Although it was a working man's vacation, I must say it was fun and I wouldn't have traded it for anything.

Although most camps with barbed wire were in operation for more than three years, I spent nearly a year outside on my own, leaving camp to go to various areas on seasonal leaves, which might have been a little different than most. Although the pay was minimal, it was better than the $12 per month we received in Fresno Assembly Center and $16 per month in Jerome. The fringe benefit was great, and we also learned a lot about the wartime ration. We found our money didn't buy sugar, meat, and other things without ration stamps, which we were unaware of being in camp.

I tried to make the best of a bad situation. With the help of my friends, I think I accomplished that.

Hachiro (Hach) Yasumura

Life in the Bayou of Jerome-Rohwer

I was five years old when we were forced to move from our home in Lomita, California. We were one of several thousand families of Japanese ancestry ordered to leave our home by the US military during World War II.

In the fall of 1942, our family of nine—Issei parents, Pop (Yasujiro), age fifty-two; Mom (Take), age forty-six; older siblings, Roy, age twenty-one; Kiku, age eighteen; Minoru (Min), age sixteen; Kengi, age fourteen; Mutsuo (Muts), age eight; me, age five; and younger brother, Hideo, age three—were transported by train (with the shades drawn) from Santa Anita Assembly Center to Jerome concentration camp (Block 20-12-B), Denson, Arkansas.

In the summer of 1944, since Jerome was closing, our family decided to move to Rohwer concentration camp (Block 24-8-CD), in Desha County, Arkansas. Both camps were located in the bayou of the Mississippi River.

The following descriptions of our life in the bayou were told by our Issei parents and my older siblings. Our oldest, Roy, was given the difficult task of being the go-between for our Issei parents—Japanese-speaking.

He was dealing with the overwhelming obstacle of explaining to our parents our forced evacuation from our home. Our camp life was very hard on our parents and on the Issei who had to give up their homes and property and leave everything behind.

Pop had arthritis and other health issues and did not work in the camp. He volunteered to help with the camp's Buddhist church along with our mom. Pop kept himself busy playing go with his newfound Japanese-speaking friends. Mom kept busy by working in the block's mess hall kitchen.

For Kiku, Min, and Kengi, teenagers, they were given the opportunity of meeting new friends, friends we would never have known if we weren't in camp. Kiku graduated from high school when we were living at the Santa Anita Assembly Center. Min and Kengi were attending high school. Min graduated in 1944 from Denson High School (Jerome). Kengi graduated in 1945 from Rohwer High School.

Yasujiro and Take. *Courtesy Roy S. Yasumura and Kengi Yasumura.*

My teenage siblings made the best of the situation while in camp. When we first arrived in Jerome in the summer of 1942, Min and Kengi and other teenage boys worked building bridges over ditches around each block before the start of high school. My older brothers and sister enjoyed listening to the music of Glenn Miller, Tommy Dorsey, Artie Shaw, and the voices of Frank Sinatra, the Andrews Sisters, the Mills Brothers, etc. They would buy *Hit Parade* and *Song Hits* magazines and memorized the words to the popular songs. Min enjoyed singing (he had a pretty good voice) and loved to draw (he was quite an artist). They went to dances, ballgames, and movies, and would pal around with their new-found friends. My sister, Kiku, enjoyed her work as a diet-aide (wearing a pink-stripe uniform) and participated in a sewing group. Min and Kengi, with friends, started a group called "Knights of 20." Roy enjoyed taking pictures with his camera.

I remember Muts saying that we all ate in a mess hall. It was cold, cold times standing in line just to get in. He also said that if you had to go to the bathroom in the middle of the night, how cold and scary that experience was. It was no fun.

Kengi shared his experience in camp. Life in camp depended on the age of the individual. For adults, the loss of freedom and the loss of your life outside the camp was disturbing. For us teenagers, we did the best we could to adapt and tried to continue our lives as it was on the outside (*shikata ga nai*—it can't be helped).

Above: The "Knights of 20" with brothers Minoru and Kengi. *Courtesy Roy S. Yasumura and Kengi Yasumura.*

Right: Roy. *Courtesy Roy S. Yasumura and Kengi Yasumura.*

Winter in Jerome was cold—snow in late December and January. We were all kept warm using a potbelly stove in each apartment. We burned wood that our mom and her friends cut for the stove in our block. Summer was very hot and very humid.

Jerome and Rohwer were like cities of their own. There were approximately thirty-five to forty blocks in each camp. Each block had about twelve barracks for living quarters, a mess hall for dining, a laundry room having connected washtubs, men's and women's bathrooms with showers, and a recreation hall. The barracks at the camp we were living in had six apartments (three different sizes—two large ones to accommodate five to six people, two medium ones for about three people, and two smaller ones for two people).

There were approximately 250 people in each block or about 8,000 in camp. Each block had a manager in charge and the mess halls were staffed by the people living in that block.

The camps were headed by the US government officials, but the office staff were internees. Under the supervision of government administrators, the security and the fire department and the hospital were also staffed by the internees. The schools (elementary, junior high, and high school) were staffed by teachers from around the nearby towns, and also by internees.

The major negative aspect of camp life was that there was no individual privacy. Families no longer were able to eat together—children met and ate with their friends in the mess hall. People had to use the same bathroom with showers with no individual stalls. Even within your own family, you lived in one large room and you put up partitions or blankets to isolate yourself.

As mentioned before, Jerome was closing and the family moved to Rohwer. That summer of 1944, Kengi joined a group of teenage boys on a work furlough to the state of Michigan. They helped harvest cherries and beans for two months.

For me and my younger brother, Hideo, we were in nursery school and kindergarten. We would sometimes tag along with our older brother, Muts. Maybe Muts was told by our parents to keep an eye on us. When we did tag along with Muts, it was usually when he was busy setting up traps to catch jackrabbits. When he caught a jackrabbit, he would sell it to this Japanese-speaking man. The man would skin it and prepared to cook the rabbit, teriyaki style. It was yummy. We were told that the same man brewed rice "sake."

One of my favorite childhood memories, while in camp, was seeing and catching fireflies and placing them in a jar during the summer nights. We were also told not to go to the creek (swampy area) because of water moccasin snakes. Some of us jumped into this huge wooden bathtub, like a small swimming pool. A Japanese-speaking man was very angry when he saw us in the tub (*ofuro*). In his broken English, he told us to wash ourselves first before entering the *ofuro*. However, for me and Hideo, our mom washed us in the laundry room, in one of those laundry washtubs.

Unfortunately, on one summer evening, I was playing with our

Right: Group photo including Minoru, Hachiro, and Hideo. *Courtesy Roy S. Yasumura and Kengi Yasumura.*

Below left: Mutsuo "Muts." *Courtesy Roy S. Yasumura and Kengi Yasumura.*

Below right: Kiku. *Courtesy Roy S. Yasumura and Kengi Yasumura.*

friends on the teeter-totter (seesaw). One of my legs got caught under the seesaw and I broke my leg. My mom came out and scolded me for staying out late. I couldn't explain to her in Japanese that something was wrong with my leg. I ended up in the hospital. Staying in the hospital wasn't so bad; my sister, Kiku, was working in the hospital and she visited me every day.

Roy, Kiku, and Min were given permission to leave camp early to seek work in Chicago, Illinois. Soon after, Roy entered the US Army and spent most of his army life with the 100th Battalion in France.

Since Roy, Kiku, and Min moved to Chicago, Kengi, age eighteen, took the responsibility (*gaman*) of looking after the rest of the family. He now had the task to be the go-between for our Issei parents. When Rohwer closed down in October 1945, Kengi moved us to Long Beach, California. We were living in a government-run trailer park. To accommodate our family of six, we lived in two trailers.

Our sincere appreciation to the many Issei and Nisei whose talents and skills allowed us to endure our life in the bayou of Jerome and Rohwer and made it more bearable.

Side note: We also had a brother, Isamu, living in Japan at the time we were in camp. In 1937, Pop took Isamu, age seven, to Japan to live with Pop's sister (at her request) in Minabe (Wakayama-ken), Japan. Isamu returned home to Long Beach in 1957. (Many of the families that were incarcerated in camp had immediate family members living in Japan during World War II.)

Ted Yenari

My Story of Ted (by Walter Imahara)

Ted T. Yenari was born on September 29, 1919, in Tacoma, Washington. His father was Daisuke Yenari (1878–1971). His mother was Kaora Sato (1887–1972).

World War II

After the outbreak of WWII, all persons of Japanese descent were moved into internment camps away from the Pacific Coast. The Yenari family, with three sons, Hajime, Susumu, and Ted, were moved to the Rohwer relocation camp in Arkansas in September 1942. After six months, the government let people leave the camp for employment in the interior. Ted relocated to Chicago to find employment. Ted joined the United States Army in Minnesota and then went for training from February to August 1944. During this period, Ted wore the same uniform that the soldiers wore at the Rohwer relocation camp. Ted volunteered for the United States Military Intelligence Service training program. In the summer of 1945, Ted completed his training and was sent overseas to the Pacific area. After serving in the Philippines and Okinawa, Ted volunteered again to join the 176th Language Detachment Headquarters, 11th Airborne Division. The Division flew into Tokyo in late August 1945, days after Japan announced its surrender. Ted served in the occupation of Japan until May 1946. He returned to Wisconsin and was honorably discharged. I asked Ted for many years about his job in the Army, but he could not tell me. Then fifty years later, Ted told me his story of being a translator.

I can remember that on the occasion of the exhibition "Behind Barbed Wire," at the National WWII Museum in 2007, Ted was honored at the reception. Ted was in his worn-out US Army uniform and was

Ted Yenari.

Ted and his wife, Tong Yenari.

in a wheelchair. A photo of Ted was placed in the exhibition, showing him in his soldier's uniform—as a soldier who had gone from Rohwer in Arkansas to Tokyo, Japan, after the ending of the war in August 1945. We were in the theater and a new film presentation was shown.

Ted has been like a brother to me all my life. Ted was our number-one family friend, starting in 1946, living in New Orleans, Louisiana, after the war. Throughout the years, until his death at the age of 94 in 2014, Ted and I shared all the good times and the bad times.

After the war, the next part of Ted's life started in New Orleans, with a degree awarded from Northern Illinois College of Optometry, Chicago, in 1948. He was on the GI Bill. With a diploma in his hand, he opened his practice of optometry in 1950. I remember going to his office on Magazine Street in downtown New Orleans. Ted was very active in business clubs, the chamber of commerce, the Veterans Association, and the National WWII Museum. Ted was the only Asian on the Mardi Gras floats, which are owned by Carnival clubs and participate in the big parades.

Ted was an athlete. He participated in the New Orleans Senior Olympics from 1991 to 2007. His specialties were the 50-meter, 100-meter, and 200-meter sprints, the high, triple, and long jumps, and of course the pole vault. And, at his size of 5'3" and 130 pounds, he was the 1995 Louisiana Games winner. Thus in 1997, Ted was inducted into the Hall of Fame of the Louisiana State Senior Olympics.

Ted wanted to be a weightlifter like me. I told Ted that he must be strong and train at least three times a week with a coach. His answer was, "Show me the two international lifts and I can do the rest." Ted had a strange training habit, but he won the 1990 US National Masters Weightlifting Championship. Ted's thinking was that he wanted to go to the 1991 World Masters Weightlifting meet in Germany with the US team. He did qualify, and I was his coach, but he never listened. He did not have any competitors in his age and body weight group and so he won a gold medal in a World competition. After the gold medal, he said that there was no challenge and it was the end of his weightlifting career. However, he would go on to win a total of seven US National Masters Championships before he actually retired from weightlifting in 2003.

Story of a Champion (by Tong Yenari)

My name is Tong Yenari. This is a long, old history of two Japanese families in Louisiana, the Imaharas and the Yenaris. It is very colorful one. Walter Imahara introduced Ted to weightlifting, but then he started other sports as well. Have you ever heard of an eighty-five-year-old pole-vaulting and high-jumping, breaking records in his age group? Ted really enjoyed the sport with the aid of Imahara-san. THAT's how he started and learned to be a good sportsman and was awarded "Sportsman of the Year." The rest is history.

Friends for Life

Ted Touru Yenari did his homework every morning, occasionally running, and practiced pole-vaulting in a friend's yard. Walter Imahara was a very good motivator-instructor. Walter enjoyed being with Ted, training and coaching him. Both always had good laughs. It was a blessing for Ted to meet Walter at his age. IMAHARA with YENARI ARE NOT just friends. Father, Mother, and the entire family were so closely knit. Ted enjoyed going to college graduations and Walter's mother's birthday party. When Mom Imahara went to the nursing home, he said he had to see her.

Masters Weightlifting

Ted enjoyed his life, always smiling, and life was always full of joy. I remember that in 1990, he won the Louisiana State Masters Weightlifting Championship. In 1991, Ted and Walter traveled to Germany for the 1991 World Masters Weightlifting Championships, and Ted won a gold

Above left: Ted Yenari (left) and a friend at the 2000 USA Track and Field National Masters Outdoor Championships in Eugene, Oregon. Ted won a gold medal by pole vaulting 6'6¾" at age eighty, and also took third in the triple jump.

Above right: Ted Yenari completing a clean-and-jerk lift in his own inimitable style.

Below: Ted winning the gold medal in Leimen, Germany, in 1991. *Photo: Walter Imahara.*

medal. He was very happy. That started his weightlifting career. Ted also participated in the Senior Olympic Games in track and field. His chest drawer is full of medals. I still have all his medals along with my children's high school trophies.

Rohwer Relocation Camp, Arkansas

Up till his nineties, his days were filled with some activity and he was always happy. He also spoke on many occasions about the Imahara family after they came from the Rohwer camp in 1945. The Yenari family went from camp to New Orleans. Ted spoke about the good times and hard times.

Louisiana

Ted spoke many times about Walter and his family living in Baton Rouge. Ted followed the Imahara family from camp to their success in the nursery and landscape business. Ted was also very close to Walter's sister Lily and her family living in St. Francisville. "God bless the Imahara family," he would say.

Ted had a great life in retirement. He was very healthy and was able to participate in many senior sports. God bless Walter and his family. I have two grown-up children. My older son, Jon, lives in Sarasota, Florida. He and his wife are doctors and they have two girls. My son Gene is an engineer who lives in Mandeville, Louisiana. He is married and has two boys.

Ted and I were blessed with our family and friends from so long ago. I am currently living in Mandeville, Louisiana.

Herbert Yomogida

My Future

As the radio spokesman announced on the radio that the West Coast was being reopened, we couldn't believe it, but we listened tensely. My mother was fixing my sister's hair, my older sister was sweeping the floor, while I was sitting near the stove. We heard this. We all at once crowded around the radio and listened. I could see our house, which was built in 1939, with its venetian blinds, our lawn with the small magnolia tree standing in the center, and our piano in the large living room with its large rug, radio, and couches. My pals Dean Kirby and Louis Harris, whom I used to play football with. Our Presbyterian Church on Locust Avenue. My new bunk bed, my junior high school and grammar school teacher. The bowling alley, the drugstore, and the store on the corner of State Street and all the old familiar places. Most of all, I wanted to go to the high school, which was so big and modern. The football games and the hikes on the beach. Yes, I was really excited. But how do I know how our neighbors will treat me after I get back? I surely hope they will treat me like they did during the prewar days. But you have to expect a few of them to be prejudiced. I surely would want to see my schoolmates. We have really changed and are grown up. Gee whiz, it doesn't seem quite true, but it really is. I just can't wait to start playing football on the grass covered lot with my old friends, whom I really missed. I bet my mother just can't wait to go back

An essay written by Herbert Yomogida when he was a student in Rohwer High School, 1942–1945. Provided, with his permission, by his sister, Joanne Okada.

to her good old cooking. But as we leave the relocation camps, I will be separated from many dear friends and teachers who helped me enjoy my stay here. I surely will miss them. My small sisters and baby brother who have practically grown up in camp will enjoy normal living. I am surely grateful for them and they will get their ice cream and candies all the time. Yes, it will help make a happy future for us.

HERBERT YOMOGIDA

Flora Imahara Yoshida

Florin, California

I am Flora Mayumi Imahara, born in 1931. This is my story on the start of a journey thru life. My father James Imahara, in 1923 at the age of twenty, bought a sixty-acre farm in Florin. The two-story redwood home had several bedrooms. The farm was just a hayfield and he paid $10,000. The land was not suitable for farming, but my father and his sister May, and her husband Yoshio, cleared the land with a horse and a plow.

I remember the farm home was big for a Japanese family in those days. My grandparents were living with us and they had a Buddhist shrine in their bedroom. In the living room, we had a grand piano, which my sister May played. May was the oldest and a smart one, and I was an average student. My father raised grapes and strawberries, but he had a vision to start raising chickens on wire in the barn. My father's thinking was that "Americans eat eggs every day and have chicken on Sunday." As the 1940s began, the Imahara family was among the most successful and prosperous families in Florin, but things quickly changed into the worst periods in our lives.

Portions of this story are reproduced with permission from the book *Family Dreams: Journey of the Sansei* (Baton Rouge, LA: 2008) by Diane Koos Gentry. Gentry carried out extensive interviews with Flora Imahara Yoshida and other family members to record their memories of the war years. This chapter, which combines new material with excerpts from Gentry's text, was compiled by Diane Yoshida Toale, the daughter of Flora Imahara Yoshida.

Pearl Harbor, December 7, 1941

My father said that he was driving with his friend, listening to the car radio on Sunday, December 7, 1941. He said the announcer broke in with the news that the Japanese bombed Pearl Harbor, Hawaii. My father said in his worst dreams the impact of this war would change our lives. My grandparents were deceased now, so they would not have to face the problems of being a Japanese. "It was a dark age," my father told the family and friends. "America was a just country and not out to hurt anyone." He desperately wanted to believe that. "I woke up one morning and it hit me," my father said; "it took the family twenty years of hard work to realize our American dream, and it was gone in an instant."

Family Number 8663

On February 19, 1942, President Franklin Roosevelt issued Executive Order 9066. It was an order to intern one hundred twenty-two thousand people of Japanese ancestry from the West Coast. No one knew if they would live or die. My mother made one of her profound statements which strikes all family members in the heart: "If we live, we live together; if we die, we'll die together." We in the family remember the statement to this day. On May 30, 1942, my parents and seven children were loaded with duffel bags labeled "8663" into a truck and headed to the Florin railroad station. (8663 was the number assigned to our family.) The train took the family to Fresno Assembly Center, a place they knew nothing about, two hundred miles away.

Fresno Assembly Center, Fresno, California

Florin, the strawberry capital of California, was a ghost town. The red strawberries were ripe in the field and ready to harvest, but there was no one to pick or market them. All the berries rotted in the field, like the spirit of the farmers who planted them. With seven children, age fifteen and below, the Imahara family boarded a train south to the Fresno Assembly Center. My father mentioned the Fresno Fairgrounds had been converted to a temporary home for five thousand exhausted, humiliated, and forgotten people of Japanese ancestry, many crying. There were acres of tar-paper barracks and horse stalls. "Soldiers herded us into the barbed-wire enclosure with bayonets," my father said. "They told us that the barbed wire was for our protection, so no one would harm us. The machine guns were also for our protection, so no one would harm us, but it was the other way, the machine guns were pointed at us."

I remember that we stayed in two horse stalls for four months. It was not for humans; it was for horses. The worst thing probably for every female was the bathrooms. The women's bathroom was just one big outhouse with lines of holes and no partitions. And the showers were wide open with no curtains.

After the shock of living in horse stables, soldiers with guns in guard towers, smelly outhouses, and Army mess hall food, there was good news. I remember that our mother, Haruka, delivered a healthy eight-pound baby boy they named Jun on June 2, 1942, just a few days after we arrived in Fresno. The family was pleased that he was born in the Fresno County Hospital, not in a horse stable. Many internees celebrated one of the first babies born in camp. A newspaper was created called the *Fresno Grapevine* for all camp residents and carried news of the birth. My father became a block manager and a translator for the Issei at a wage of $19 a month. Sister May, the oldest in the family at fourteen, got a job typing. The children were always well fed, never hungry. "Nothing can keep the Japanese SPIRIT down for long," my father said. "Evacuation and camp life were low points in our lives, but they were so low, we knew we'd hit bottom and could only go up. The spirit is in our hearts."

Internment in Jerome, Arkansas

In October 1942, less than five months after arriving in Fresno, the family and others in camp were told to pack up. They would be going to their permanent relocation camp, prison camp, concentration camp, or internment camp as some called it—Camp Jerome. The camp was deep in the Arkansas swamps, two thousand miles away from home. Our long black train with five hundred people left Fresno for Jerome. All families wondered if they would ever see friends and family again. All internees were herded on the trains by soldiers. The shades were pulled down on each window, but we all peeked through the cracks. For the four-day, five-night train ride to Arkansas, the ride was roughest on my mother with eight children and one still breastfeeding.

The train arrived at Jerome and the internees saw all the swampland covered with shrubs and trees. A lot of rumors of the huge mosquitoes, rattlesnakes, and alligators were heard. The camp was not ready, and the

tar-paper barracks were still under
construction. The kitchen staff
had no meals to prepare for seven
thousand people. Our family was
the biggest family in camp and was
assigned two rooms, each twenty
by twenty feet, in the hundred-
foot-long tar-paper barracks. Each
room had a single light hanging and
a metal potbelly stove. Inside were
cots with straw mattresses, nothing
else.

I, Flora, was age twelve, and
remember some details about the
camps; the whole experience tore
me apart. I thought I was Japanese,
and I think I took it personally
when the Japanese bombed Pearl

Flora Imahara's name on the memo-
rial plaque (at top) at the Fresno
Assembly Center. *Photo: Walter
Imahara.*

Harbor and started the war. I was put into camp; therefore, I must be bad.
It crushed my self-identity, I didn't want to be Japanese, and I wanted to
be white. If I was white, then I'd be acceptable. For years I wondered why
the Japanese went to camp and not the Germans or Italians. I got more
and more angry and used foul language in camp. I didn't understand and
could not resolve my anger until I was thirty-eight years old.

Rohwer Relocation Center

In April of 1944, my mother had to move the family to the Rohwer
internment camp, twenty miles away, so the Army could bring German
prisoners to Jerome. The camp looked and functioned just like Jerome.
What differed was the neighbors in this camp were suffering far greater
tragedies; many of them had yellow telegrams delivered to their doors.
We found out many years later that the Blue Star on the barracks door
meant that a member of the family was serving in the US Army. The Gold
Star meant a member of the family had passed away, giving his life for
his country, while the family was behind barbed wire. I remembered the
yellow telegrams in camp and understood what was happening. I thought,
"Wasn't camp enough punishment? They went to war and did their job,
many giving their lives for a country that hated them. And their parents

or loved ones were behind barbed wire. They were loyal Americans." We heard crying all over the camp, it was so sad.

At Rohwer, the camp was the same as Jerome: barbed wire, guard towers, communal bathrooms, mess halls. I remember that the family unity was breaking down. The children ate with their friends and the older folks ate together. The children had a good time playing baseball and going to school. In August 1944, the wartime authorities removed all barriers and allowed Japanese American students to leave camp to go to college. But restrictions remained for the West Coast. The fences fell and we played on the guard towers. No one escaped as there was no place to go. We still had the face of the enemy.

World War II Is Over

On August 6, 1945, at 8:15 a.m., President Truman ordered the atomic bomb dropped on Hiroshima and, on August 9, on Nagasaki. The war was over on August 25, 1945. My grandfather, Minezo Imahara, Issei, was born in Hiroshima in 1857 and came to America in 1895. My mother, who once lived in Hiroshima, was stunned and hurt when she heard about the bombs. "Why do people do war?" she asked. "They should use their minds to make peace."

New Orleans, Louisiana

My parents researched to locate a proper area to which to move, knowing they would be leaving camp one day. My mother wanted to relocate to the South where the people would be friendlier than in California. The government would give only $25 for each family member to start a new life, or a total of $250. My parents decided New Orleans would be a large enough city to have jobs for my father. My mother heard that Louisiana had many fine colleges. More than anything, this influenced her decision. Education was the one thing no one could take away from you. They could take your farm, your freedom, and your livelihood, but not your education. She knew in her heart that her children would succeed in any career if they had a college education. My mother was the voice and decision maker for our family. All nine children would go to Mom for any problems and she would solve them with a clear mind. She saw to it that the children would get a good education. Sister May went to business school, and the eight other children eventually got a college education.

Left: Flora Imahara in New Orleans, Louisiana, 1946. Flora is holding the embroidery she created during her time in Rohwer, 1944–45.

Right: Flora in Saratoga, California, in February 2020, holding the same embroidery shown in the previous photo.

"I wanted to start a new life without discrimination," my father said. "We had no problems renting. Maybe in New Orleans, all the prejudice would be toward the Blacks and we would not be the bad guys. Maybe they didn't know about the war or Japan. Maybe they will just ignore us." We were dead wrong. Mom said the hardest time in New Orleans was the struggle to buy food, but people were kind. Pop said, "After the war in New Orleans, I crawled, and I cried."

I recalled my parents speaking about the Japanese family unity breaking down in camp. The family did not dine together in the mess hall. After arriving in New Orleans, we slept on newspaper and the first furniture purchased was a round table. No one sat at the head of the table and we had our meals at a given time. We faced each other and there was only one topic: EDUCATION. There was no other topic and we children grew tired of hearing about it. But we understood the message and when we all went to college, we were so grateful for the sacrifice of our parents.

My father found work in a chicken hatchery tending incubators all night. He made $50 a week, barely enough to pay the rent. Then he worked in a laundry and did carpentry—always jobs in which he was not seen by the public. By 1945, sister May, the oldest in the family at age twenty, worked part time as a sales clerk while finishing business school. When store managers sang the old refrain, "We don't hire Japs," she bravely started writing "white" as her race on job applications, never going without a job after that. She made $11 a week and gave half to the family. The family remembers that both of our parents wanted us to go to college, but it was Mom who insisted that all the girls in the family would have a college education. We went to Mom with all our personal problems and need for money. Because of the emphasis on education, it really didn't matter if we were a minority or a poor family in a poor state. All the children had goals, and how we thrived. This story I will never forget: eight children went to college and all four boys JOINED the service and returned safely.

It was at the age of thirty-eight that I came to truly accept myself as God's child through my growing relationship with Jesus Christ, my Lord and Savior. Through my years of studying the Bible, I was blessed to teach God's word to women from all walks of life and ethnicities. For the past fifty years, I have put Christ first in my life and have been blessed abundantly. I grew to understand God's sovereignty; He created me exactly as He wanted me to be, a Japanese American woman. God's plan was perfect and He used my camp experience to share His love and plan of salvation to my family and each person He brought into my life. I hold no bitterness towards anyone for the terrible loss and suffering our family endured. I know that God was and is always in control of our lives and I have freedom in knowing His true love and acceptance. At my father's age of ninety-six and before his passing, I had the honor and privilege of bringing him to Christ after many years of praying for his salvation.

Dan O. Yoshii

George and Helen Yoshii Family Story

I was born at Rohwer, much too young back then to remember anything about the internment or camp life. The Yoshii family (Barracks 2-3-C), after more than three years of imprisonment, returned to Los Angeles, and settled near Torrance, California.

Life was simple in those early years after the war. Our father, a former businessman, decided to try farming wholesale flowers, mainly carnations. I do remember him saying he knew nothing about growing flowers other than sticking them in the ground and watering them. Those were challenging years to start over again with basically nothing, except determination; we adapted, our family survived. With pride, our parents made sure we received a college education.

Little was spoken about the internment, as the subject wasn't of much interest to young children and not taught in schools. When family friends from camp days would visit, there were adult conversations about Rohwer. Our parents never expressed anger, but others certainly did!

I grew up knowing little about camp life at Rohwer, though our parents would have openly answered any questions, if only we would have asked; that was in their nature as Nisei pioneers, they were all-American! Our mom, Helen Yoshii, made the best apple pie!

I remember being told our dad, George Yoshii, was chief of Rohwer Police, at least for a time. He had use of a jeep, could leave camp, and could travel to nearby McGehee. Jack May, former mayor, City of McGehee, revealed in 2012, "Just recently some people were searching for Indian arrowheads in a cotton field about six miles from the Rohwer camp and found this [police] badge. They cleaned it up and it is in beautiful condition." The Rohwer Police badge artifact is in possession of the

Left: Rohwer Police Station in 1944. George Yoshii seated left; Burt Clayton seated right (with cigar). Note the police badge on their shirts.

Below: Rohwer Police Station. George Yoshii is seated in the front row, fifth from left.

World War II Japanese American Internment Museum in McGehee, Arkansas.

Mayor May identified Burt Clayton, Chief of the Internal Security force, with his signature cigar. The former mayor had a family connection to local civilian law enforcement during the war and tells of visiting Rohwer as a youngster.

If anyone has documentation or memories of George Yoshii being a chief of Rohwer Police, we'd appreciate knowing for sure, and send any details to the museum in McGehee.

Amache, Granada Relocation Center, Colorado

I have visited Rohwer twice, many years ago. It is much too far away for me to visit, now retired. Amache (Granada Relocation Center), Colorado, is about a three-hour drive from my home, yet I've been there only a handful of times. I have enjoyed working (long distance) with the Amache Preservation Society, consisting of students at Granada High School, mainly by internet, for over twenty years.

Amache and Rohwer do have another thing in common: they both are near the Arkansas River. The Arkansas has its headwaters in central Colorado, high up in the Rockies, passes about two miles north of Granada, runs through Little Rock, and joins the Mississippi River a few miles north of Rohwer. The two camps are connected . . . by a river!

Accounts from
Mary Kawakami, Hank Umemoto,
and Elaine Francis Wilson

MARY KAWAKAMI

*Joanne Okada, a former Rohwer internee, has an older rela-
tive named Mary Kawakami, who currently lives in Highland,
Utah. Mary recently recalled her experiences during World War
II when she was living in American Fork, Utah. She is now
108 years young, an alert, strong, intelligent, and elegant lady,
and her birthday was December 12. Mary has the unique birth
numbers of 12-12-12. She was prominently known and recognized as a businesswoman in her community of Provo, Utah.
In fact, she has a street named for her on the Main Street exit
in American Fork. This story was told by Mary to a caregiver
named Dana, who wrote it out in Mary's own words. Joanne
Okada assisted in the interview.*

December 7, 1941. During the war, many Japanese were placed in concentration camps but because we lived in the interior of the US, we didn't
have to go to the concentration camps. Most of the Japanese in the area
were farmers or worked at the Pulley's Turkey Farm. They were treated

Mary
Kawakami.

well and fairly at the turkey farm as many of us were permitted to work there, so many worked there.

But that didn't mean that there wasn't any concern about the loyalty of the Japanese citizens. There were some individuals who truly believed that their Japanese neighbors would sneak into their homes and cut their throats in their beds because of all the propaganda that was out there.

One woman was so public in her prejudice that her own husband apologized for her behavior. She was the liaison between the Red Cross and the Japanese Americans in Utah. She would withhold information that should have been given to them immediately. She was sent an expedited letter to advise that a Japanese American serviceman had been killed in action. She didn't contact his family. She said, "It doesn't matter to me."

I had two FBI agents visit me two days after returning home from the hospital after the birth of my daughter, Marilyn. They wanted to search the house for contraband. There was no visible contraband, but we had some photographic equipment to take pictures of our children and a flashlight. So, while the FBI agents (one tall man and one short man) were looking through the house, I took these things and put them in the toilet in the outhouse. I was afraid of these FBI men and what they would do to us if they found them. It was a shame to lose the flashlight because we needed it to see at night when we were irrigating water in the fields. The FBI agents started questioning me why I had so many bottles of canned fruits and vegetables. I had about a hundred bottles. He asked me, "Who told you to keep so much food? What are you keeping it for?" I answered that we were told by our church to prepare for the future and to keep food storage. I didn't know how to can, but one woman who was very nice to me had helped and taught me how. Her father was a leader of the Church of Jesus Christ of Latter-day Saints. Her husband was the president of the local bank and he told me that he would make sure no one would bother us for being Japanese. And no one did. One time, he and his wife decided that we needed some culture and they took me and my husband to a music concert sponsored by the church. They sat on each side of us so that we were protected from anyone who might have objected to our being there.

Prejudice didn't begin during the war, however. When I was in school in Murray, they were having a speech contest. First place would win a watch. My sister Smiley was very excited. She wanted to win that watch! She worked very hard and titled her speech "Why I Love America." The day came and she gave her speech. All the teachers were impressed. They said that she won first place. But the superintendent (his name was Clove) said he couldn't give first place to a Jap. He would give her second place. She was furious and said that she wanted the first place, since she earned it. But he awarded it to a white American. The teachers were appalled that an educator would be that way. Later, when my sister was sixteen, she won first place in a sewing and design contest at the same school. One day my sixteen-year-old sister got on a bus and a woman asked her, "You're a Jap, aren't you?" My sister, indignant, retorted, "I am an American, what are you?" Other people on the bus applauded her.

This is my story. —MARY KAWAKAMI, age 108

HANK UMEMOTO

Hank Umemoto was a classmate and friend of Jerome-Rohwer internee May Imahara when they lived in California before the war. Here he recalls the postcards he received from May during the war, when he was interned at the Manzanar Relocation Center in California.

Always, May

Yellow mustard plants amid the flourishing barn grass now covered the vineyard where California poppy once displayed its golden splendor. It was the final days of spring and California poppy was wilting like the Tokay grape farmers who came to this country and toiled for over three decades. It was the final chapter for the Japanese immigrants who

May Imahara. *Imahara photo.*

came here, where money grew on trees. But the end to their hopes and dreams arrived during the winter of 1942, when FDR issued Executive Order 9066 that mandated that everyone of Japanese ancestry, US citizens or not, is forcibly removed from the West Coast.

I was thirteen years old at the time, living in a predominantly Japanese community which we proudly called Taisho-ku [Florin, California], and was a seventh grader at Sierra Grammar School located on Hedge Road South of Jackson Road (Hwy 16). There were twelve students in our class. Three were white boys; four were Sansei (third-generation Japanese), namely May Imahara, Florence Wakita, Carolyn Abe, and Herb Umeda; and five were Nisei (second-generation Japanese), namely Fred Taniguchi, Moosey Hisamoto, Sam Sakai, Eric Tanikawa, and myself. We were a tightly knit group where we grew up together, studied together, played together, and attended Taisho-Gakuen, a Japanese-language school situated on the southeast corner of Hedge Avenue and Fruitridge Avenue, for one hour after our American school. (California law permitted Japanese language to be taught no more than five hours a week.)

Hank Umemoto at Manzanar in front of his barrack shortly before departing for Los Angeles, 1945. *Photo courtesy Hank Umemoto Collection.*

Finally, the day arrived when we were to depart for some faraway places which we never heard of and were not even on the map. I helped board up the windows and nail down the doors, while Mother drenched her vegetable garden with water, and fed the last meal to her chickens, not knowing when we would return to our home or even if we would return at all. We silently performed our final chores, drenched in a sea of gloom and despair. But for a thirteen-year-old teenager, my friends were my universe and to be separated from them was also one of the most depressing moments of my life. May, Florence, Fred, Moosey, and Sam were sent to Fresno Assembly Center and later to Jerome Relocation Center, then eventually to Rohwer Relocation Center in Arkansas. Carolyn and Herb were sent to Pinedale Assembly Center in Fresno, California. Eric and I went to Manzanar Relocation Center in California.

Almost all my Taisho-ku friends and lifelong friends from Manzanar are long gone but the memory still lingers on. I still remember a postcard addressed to "Hank Umemoto, Manzanar, California" and even to date, I marvel at the efficiency of the United States Postal Service of yesteryear. The postcard said that they are at Fresno Assembly Center and everyone is fine and wrapped up with a simple, "Always, May." Perhaps that is an appropriate ending, since I always remember those eight classmates

APPENDIX   207

Hank Umemoto (1928–2019). Hank is showing his book, *Manzanar to Mount Whitney: The Life and Times of a Lost Hiker* (Berkeley, CA: Heyday, 2013). *Photo courtesy Mario Gershom Reyes/Rafu Shimpo.*

whom I grew up with at Sierra School, always like brothers and sisters, always cherishing the wonderful days we shared and who will always remain dear to my heart. May probably would not mind if I paraphrase her and conclude the chronicle with:

ALWAYS,
HANK UMEMOTO

ELAINE FRANCIS WILSON

Elaine Francis Wilson, born in 1948 in Watsonville, California, grew up within the large Japanese American community there; later she moved to Louisiana. Here she recounts to Walter Imahara some of her childhood recollections.

Dear Mr. Imahara,

I sit with tears in my eyes reading of your family history. I truly thought of the Imahara family over the years. I never realized we lived in the same towns.

I too am from Watsonville, California. My love, my family's love for the Japanese people has always been so very strong. With tears I remember my junior high school teacher, Mas Hashimoto, and his goal to have compensation to the Japanese families that lost everything due to World War II.

My father refused the gun position the Navy had placed him in. It was WWII, he was sixteen. The Navy moved him to the cook's position. It was hard for children that grew up knowing the Japanese that lived around them. It was also so very hard to see them lose all they had worked so hard for and be put in camps far from their home.

I was born there in 1948. Many Japanese had farms around the coastal area of Watsonville and north of Santa Cruz. One of my favorite stories was about my father and his grandfather going to the San Francisco World's Fair. The amazing sights they saw! They, like many, had very little money, yet my great-grandfather wanted my dad to see what the future for him would hold.

At the time, my great-aunt and family raised Brussels sprouts in Davenport. One neighbor up the coast was a Japanese family. They sold their only cow in order to have money to go to the San Francisco World's Fair. A neighbor asked them why they would sell their only cow. The Japanese farmer said they could live without the cow, but they could not live without the education that the World's Fair would give them.

I went to school with many Japanese and always looked forward to the teriyaki chicken dinners at the Watsonville Buddhist Temple. I worked with pharmacist Mr. Ben Umeda. And I loved the beautiful landscape and flower displays at the Santa Cruz County Fair there in Watsonville.

The Imahara name was so familiar when we moved to Baton Rouge in 1974. Yet I had no idea you could possibly have come from my hometown. Life has been busy with children, grandchildren, and a great-granddaughter. I sat to finally read about Mr. Imahara, who had designed a beautiful botanical garden so close to Baton Rouge.

With tears I remember childhood and life long ago. This was a place I longed to see, but had not been there yet. A place of peace and solitude and beauty that I remember from childhood in Watsonville. I pray we will get up to meet you and see the handiwork that will grow more and more beautiful each year. You have planted it for the many tomorrows yet to come. What an awesome gift and legacy you have created. I truly hope the new owners from time to time will allow your family to visit and see the beauty created. That your family will understand the generations that all they see represents.

In Watsonville all Japanese were known for beautiful yards. So in tune with nature. Thank you for all the time, all the years of your life that have resulted in so much beauty.

Truly hope to see and to meet you before April 29th.

Very Sincerely,
Elaine (Francis) Wilson

INDEX

Identification of individuals as "internee" is based on available information.

at Rohwer Relocation Center, 51, 86, 120

at Tule Lake Relocation Center, 53

WWII Japanese American Internment Museum (McGehee, AR). *See* Japanese American Internment Museum

Yada family, 122

Yamada family, 32, 44

Yamamoto, Mits (internee), 177–79
photos, 178, 179

Yasumura family. *See also specific family members*
at Jerome Relocation Center, 180–85
relocations, 184–85
at Rohwer Relocation Center, 180
at Santa Anita Assembly Center, 180

Yasumura, Hachiro (Hach) (internee), 180–85
photo, 184

Yasumura, Hideo (internee), 180, 183
photo, 184

Yasumura, Isamu, 185

Yasumura, Kengi (internee), 180, 181, 183
photo, 182

Yasumura, Kiku (internee), 180, 181
photo, 184

Yasumura, Minoru (Min) (internee), 180, 181, 183
photo, 182, 184

Yasumura, Mutsuo (Muts) (internee), 180, 181
photo, 184

Yasumura, Roy (internee), 180, 181
photo, 182

Yasumura, Take (internee), 180
photo, 181

Yasumura, Yasujiro (internee), 180
photo, 181

yellow telegrams, 63

Yenari family. *See also specific family members*
in New Orleans, 190
at Rohwer Relocation Center, 186
in Tacoma, WA, 186

Yenari, Daisuke (internee), 186

Yenari, Gene, 190

Yenari, Hajime (internee), 186

Yenari, Jon, 190

Yenari, Susumu (internee), 186

Yenari, Ted (internee), 186–90
photos, 187, 189

Yenari, Tong, 188
photo, 187

Yomogida family. *See also specific family members*
at Jerome Relocation Center, 22–23
in Long Beach, CA, 21
at Rohwer Relocation Center, 22–23
at Santa Anita Assembly Center, 21–22

Yomogida, Evelyn (internee), 21

Yomogida, George (internee), 21, 23, 24

Yomogida, Glenn (internee), 24

Yomogida, Harold, 24

Yomogida, Herbert (internee), 21, 191–92

Yomogida, Janet (internee), 21–24
photos, 22, 108

Yomogida, Joanne (internee), 21, 63, 107–9
photos, 64, 108, 109

Yomogida, Ruth (internee), 21, 23, 24

Yoshida, Flora Imahara. *See* Imahara, Flora (internee)

Yoshii, Dan O. (internee), 200–202

Yoshii, George (internee), 200
photos, 201

Yoshii, Helen (internee), 200

Yoshikawa, Fred, 43

Yoshimura family, 122

Yoshizaki, Tetsuo (internee), 51

INDEX

WALTER M. IMAHARA was born in California, where his family were prominent members of the local Japanese American farming community before World War II. After being interned at Jerome and Rohwer, he became a US Army officer, the owner of a successful nursery and landscape business, and a national champion weightlifter. He is the author of *I Am an American: Japanese American, Asian Cajun.*

DAVID E. MELTZER is associate professor in the College of Integrative Sciences and Arts at Arizona State University in Mesa.